BLOODAXE CONTEMPORARY FRENCH POETS

Throughout the twentieth century, France has been a dominant force in the development of European culture. It has made essential contributions and advances not just in literature but in all the arts, from the novel to film and philosophy; in drama (Theatre of the Absurd), art (Cubism and Surrealism) and literary theory (Structuralism and Post-Structuralism). These very different art forms and intellectual modes find a dynamic meeting-point in post-war French poetry.

Some French poets are absorbed by the latest developments in philosophy or psychoanalysis. Others explore relations between poetry and painting, between the written word and the visual image. There are some whose poetry is rooted in Catholicism, and others who have remained faithful to Surrealism, and whose poetry is bound to a life of action or political commitment.

Because it shows contemporary French poetry in a broader context, this new series will appeal both to poetry readers and to anyone with an interest in French culture and intellectual life. The books themselves also provide an imaginative and exciting approach to French poets which makes them ideal study texts for schools, colleges and universities.

Each volume is a single, unabridged collection of poems presented in a parallel-text format, with the French text facing an English verse translation by a distinguished expert or poet-translator. The editor of each book is an authority on the particular writer, and in each case the editor's introduction presents not only a critical appreciation of the work and its place in the author's output but also a comprehensive account of its social, intellectual and cultural background.

The series itself has been planned in such a way that the individual volumes will build up into a stimulating and informative introduction to contemporary French poetry, giving readers both an intimate experience of how French poets think and write, and a working overview of what makes poetry important in France.

BLOODAXE CONTEMPORARY FRENCH POETS

Series Editors: Timothy Mathews & Michael Worton

Timothy Mathews is Professor of French at University College London. His books include *Reading Apollinaire: Theories of Poetic Language* (Manchester University Press, 1987 & 1990) and *Literature, Art and the Pursuit of Decay in 20th Century France* (CUP, 2000). He co-edited *Tradition, Translation, Trauma: The Classic and the Modern* (OUP, 2011) with Jan Parker, and co-translated Luce Irigaray's *Prières quotidiennes/Everyday Prayers* (Larose/University of Nottingham Press, 2004) with Irigaray. The first volume in this series, *On the Motion and Immobility of Douve* by Yves Bonnefoy, has an introduction by him.

Michael Worton was Vice-Provost and Fielden Professor of French Language and Literature at University College London. He has published extensively on contemporary French writers, with two books on Michel Tournier, and co-edited *Intertextuality* (1990), *Textuality and Sexuality* (1993), *Women's Writing in Contemporary France* (2003), *National Healths: Gender, Sexuality and Health in a Cross-Cultural Context* (2004), *Liberating Learning* (2010) and *French Studies in and for the 21st Century* (2011). The second volume in the Bloodaxe Contemporary French Poets series, *The Dawn Breakers* by René Char, is introduced and translated by him.

BLOODAXE CONTEMPORARY FRENCH POETS: 5

PHILIPPE JACCOTTET

Under Clouded Skies AND Beauregard

Pensées sous les nuages ET Beauregard

Translated by
DAVID CONSTANTINE
& MARK TREHARNE

Introduction by
MARK TREHARNE

BLOODAXE BOOKS

BLOODAXE CONTEMPORARY FRENCH POETS: 5
Philippe Jaccottet: *Under Clouded Skies / Beauregard*

Original French text of *Pensées sous les nuages*
by Philippe Jaccottet © Éditions Gallimard 1983.
English translation © David Constantine & Mark Treharne 1994.
Original French text of *Beauregard*
by Philippe Jaccottet © Éditions Gallimard 1984.
English translation © Mark Treharne 1994.
Introduction © Mark Treharne 1994.

ISBN: 978 1 85224 259 6

This edition published 1994 by
Bloodaxe Books Ltd,
Eastburn,
South Park,
Hexham,
Northumberland NE46 1BS.

www.bloodaxebooks.com
For further information about Bloodaxe titles
please visit our website and join our mailing list
or write to the above address for a catalogue.

Supported by
ARTS COUNCIL
ENGLAND

Bloodaxe Books Ltd, the translators and the series editors,
wish to thank the Ministère des Affaires Étrangères, Paris,
and the Service Culturel, the French Embassy, London,
for their assistance and for help given towards translation costs.

Digital reprint of the 1994 edition.

CONTENTS

Pensées sous les nuages (1983)

Beauregard (1981)

Pensées sous les nuages (1983)

Beauregard (1981)

GENERAL EDITORS' PREFACE

The Bloodaxe Contemporary French Poets series aims to bring a broad range of post-war French poetry to as wide an English-speaking readership as possible, and it has specific features which are designed to further this aim.

First of all, each volume is devoted to a complete, unabridged work by a poet. This is designed to maintain the coherence of what a poet is trying to achieve in publishing a book of poems. We hope that in this way, the particular sense of a poet working within language will be highlighted. Secondly, each work appears in parallel translation. Finally, each work is prefaced by a substantial essay which gives a critical appreciation of the book of poetry, of its place in its author's work, as well as an account of its social and intellectual context.

In each case, this essay is written by an established critic with a love of French poetry. It aims not only to be informative, but also to respond in a lively and distinctive way to the pleasures and challenges of reading each poet. Similarly, the translators, often poets in their own right, adopt a range of different approaches, and in every case they seek out an English that gives voice to the uniqueness of the French poems.

Each translation in the series is not just faithful to the original, but aims to recreate the poet's voice or its nearest equivalent in another language: each is a translation from French poetry into English poetry. Each essay seeks to make its own statement about how and why we read poetry and think poetry. The work of each poet dovetails with others in the series to produce a living illustration of the importance of poetry in contemporary French culture.

T.M.
M.W.

INTRODUCTION

Philippe Jaccottet was born in Switzerland (Moudon, Vaud) in 1925. He studied literature in Lausanne between 1944 and 1946. From 1946 to 1953 he worked in Paris for a Swiss publisher and during this period made his first visits to Italy (a country and a culture of considerable importance to him). Since 1953, the year of his marriage to the painter Anne-Marie Haesler, he has lived in France in Grignan (Drôme) earning his living as a translator and writing. In addition to poetry, Jaccottet has published a variety of prose writings, notebooks and critical essays. He is particularly well known as a translator from German (Musil, Rilke, Thomas Mann, Hölderlin) but has also translated Homer, Plato, Ungaretti, Montale, Góngora and Mandelstam among many others. He has won many distinguished prizes for his work both in France and elsewhere.

Under clouded skies (1983) and *Beauregard* (1980) are relatively late collections in Jaccottet's writing career. Before treating them individually and indicating some of their distinctive features, I want to give a broader picture of Jaccottet's writing and to provide a context in which they can be placed.

I. *Presences and Absences*

> ... la lampe allumée
> sur l'interminable lecture
> (... the lamp lit
> on unending reading)
> – PHILIPPE JACCOTTET: *Airs*

This introduction is primarily an invitation to read two texts by Jaccottet. I shall therefore begin with the inspection of a particular poem.

Là où la terre s'achève	Where earth ends
levée au plus près de l'air	lifted nearest to air
(dans la lumière où le rêve	(in the light where the invisible
invisible de Dieu erre)	dream of God strays)
entre pierre et songerie	between stone and dream
cette neige: ermine enfuie	this snow: vanished ermine
	(*Airs*)

This poem focusses on snow contemplated at a distance, on a mountain height at a confine between earth and sky. It is brief and elliptical, an icon of the elusive kind of sign encountered in a landscape, a 'fugitive inscription', as Jaccottet puts it in *Paysages avec figures absentes / Landscapes with absent figures*. It opts for a minimal language, brevity of metre and a particular use of blank space. Sparsely punctuated and separated into three segments by blanks, it can nonetheless be read as a syntactically coherent sentence with a main verb implied. The sentence is structured in a series of balanced pairings: lines 1 and 2 are equated with 3 and 4 as notations of place ('Là où...'/'dans la lumière où...') and line 5 extends this notion and proposes another 'place' between 'pierre' and 'songerie'. 'Pierre' associates itself with 'terre' of the first line conceptually and phonically; similarly 'rêve' and 'songerie' are conceptually linked, but the rhyme with 'achève' inflects the former with a negative suggestion of finality. The final line of the poem, with its strong break at the colon, creates a balance from the obvious linkage of 'neige' and 'ermine' (snow white as ermine), but at the same time effects a forceful contrast between the demonstrative 'cette' and the absence indicated by 'enfuie'. It is a bewildering deixis, this pointing at an absence. Where is the poem "taking place"?

We have a sentence which on a grammatical level does not strike us as a splintered or particularly ambiguous structure: it has a syntactical logic which seems to assert its way to meaning. The organisation of the sentence into a poem of seven-syllable lines and into a pattern of rhyme suggests formal coherence: there are again balanced pairings (the rhyming pattern is ab/ab; lines 5 and 6 have a phonic ressemblance, although the rhyme is only a half-rhyme). At the same time this structure is a light and even tenuous one. The rhyme is extremely supple, it does not call attention to itself: the strong *enjambement* at lines 3/4 and the break at the colon in line 6 attenuates any effect of laboured formality. The dramatic apex of the poem is the last line: the strong pause at the colon creates a point of focus on 'cette neige'. Grammatically the colon leads us to expect equivalence, but the equivalence is highly enigmatic semantically because it equates a presence with an absence.

The poem is also given a distinctive layout: three segments which suggest three different stages in a process of awareness. In the first, there is an insistence on distance and altitude, followed by a parenthesis which parallels the first two lines but converts what is registered as external space into the internalised space of imaginative association. Yet the parenthesis can also be read as conferring a provisional status upon its contents, signifying a possibility. And if we read 'erre' in both its senses ('strays' / 'is mistaken'), there is

10

already ambiguity. The second segment is posed between the tangible and the seen on the one hand ('pierre') and the intangible and invisible ('songerie') on the other. The third segment then focusses upon the object of attention, the snow, in what appears to be a concrete notation before this is exploded in the final image. Words and their meanings are playing a teasing and ambivalent game.

A further and immediately striking feature is that the poem plays constantly on the phonetic unit [ɛr]. This phonic recurrence chimes with the title of the collection from which the poem comes, *Airs* [ɛr]. Yet the word is semantically pluralistic: it encompasses 'air' (the element), 'tunes' or 'songs', and 'appearances'. The phonic recurrence [ɛr] in the poem signals what we might think of as its musicality, but the string of semantic possibilities, like musical sound itself, refuses to be entirely "decidable".

This six-line poem, then, is articulated with some complexity. It creates a pattern of distances and tensions between presence and absence, the visible and the invisible, the present and the past. It hesitates on a number of levels. The absence of a main verb – and the invitation to supply one – leaves us full of questions. Who is noting this? Why is the subject effaced in this way? What we are left with is an enigmatic verbal landscape that seems to allude to physical landscape, but we are not sure. Perhaps this is the point. The laconic style provokes an involvement with the poem that a more explicit formulation would not have done. To what sort of context does such writing belong?

II. *Figures in a Landscape*

...nature – or what we call nature: the collection of objects and processes which surround us and which in turn engender and devour us – is no more our accomplice than she is our confidante.
     – OCTAVIO PAZ, *The Monkey Grammarian*

With its extremely subtle acidic reactions, the eye, an organ possessed of hearing...intensifies the value of the image...raises the picture to its own level; for painting is much more a matter of internal secretion than of apperception, that is, of external perceiving.
     – OSIP MANDELSTAM, *Journey to Armenia*

Jaccottet's texts are animated by a fascination with the visible world, and largely, but not exclusively, with a specific locality, the Drôme which is situated just north of Provence. The Drômois landscape is the pretext for the major part of Jaccottet's poetry. This is an elective site and Jaccottet has made a deliberate move away from 'l'ébranlement des villes' / 'the commotion of the city' in the conviction that the lot of the modern poet is exclusion and solitude, that a poetic response to the world is a studied and centred act of attention and meditation. Distraction is inimical to a project which aims to articulate responses to the elemental realities encountered in the natural cycle, as if these provided a lesson too readily neglected by modernity and too easily relegated to clichés of Romantic "nature poetry". The near exclusion of the urban and the industrial from Jaccottet's texts might seem anachronistic to some; certainly, questions do, and should arise about the viability of "nature poetry" in a world where there are arguably more urgent claims to attention. The trouble with the expression "nature poetry" is that, in a naive view, it inevitably invokes notions like pathetic fallacy, the cultivation of idyll and indulgent escapism. These are liabilities of which Jaccottet is certainly aware and from which he is at pains to distance himself. To understand how he does so, we need to turn from the matter to the manner of his inspection.

While the elements of a specific place do matter (for instance, they anchor most of the writing in a circumscribed landscape, a recognisable world, the better to focus the attention), this is not writing that signifies 'the Drôme', or at least only tangentially so. It needs to be made clear from the start that we are not dealing with a "regional writer" or with an art of the picturesque: nor is this a merely descriptive poetic. The landscapes in question provide a point of focus for sensory, affective and meditative response. One of the most richly suggestive of Jaccottet's titles (it belongs to a prose text central to an understanding of his writing) is the ambiguous *Paysages avec figures absentes / Landscapes with absent figures*. It lures us in the direction of visual representation, towards landscape painting. The preposition 'avec' / 'with' reinforces the pictural sense by invoking models like 'Landscape with bathers'. But the qualifying adjective 'absentes' undermines this fiction and problematises, but does not obliterate, any obvious sense of relation with painting. This is a paradoxical formulation of absence and presence. The visual focus of Jaccottet's writing is implicitly paralleled with the work of the painter but at the same time this title holds in check any facile identification of the verbal and the visual. The landscapes of *Paysages avec figures absentes* are transpositions of the optical, mediations in a verbal semiosis or process of signification (hence one sense of 'absentes': the figures as they might be depicted by the painter are simply not there). 'Figures' (already ambiguous: faces? people? shapes? etc) is therefore orientated towards figures of writing rather than towards mediations through the brush and palette. These questions are exemplified by the painters Jaccottet has occasionally worked with in the production of a text, notably Tal Coat and Zao Wou-ki: their work is nonfigurative but suggests traces of figurative representation and has accompanied Jaccottet's texts not as "illustration" of them but as visual analogue. The result of these collaborations are books which juxtapose the visual and the verbal sign, and they make their own distinctive contribution to the larger enquiry about the relation of the visual to the verbal, endemic in modern French poetry at least since Baudelaire.

So while naturalistic elements of locality have their place in his writing, what matters more is the fact that Jaccottet uses the natural world to conduct a scrupulous record of the experience of the eye, of attentiveness, both pushed to their limits. His observations exceed the merely optical and have much to convey about the ramifications of visual perception such as we find them explored in the work of Maurice Merleau-Ponty or John Berger. In the conclusion to *L'Entretien des muses / The Parley of the Muses*, Jaccottet describes much of recent French poetry as a meticulous inventory of the visible conducted with so much attentiveness that it inevitably comes up against the limits of the visible. This is the case with his own project. A notebook entry reads: 'How strange the eyes are: they drink in the world and contribute to its metamorphosis into immaterial images, or less material ones...' (*La Semaison / Seedtime*: entry for March 1976). This is one version of a process which Jaccottet's writing transcribes and which ultimately, on a good day, results in the poem.

While the objects in a landscape remain naturalistically "themselves" and are scrupulously recorded as such, they also figure consistently in Jaccottet's work as objects of meditation and metaphoric potential (mountain, bird, tree, flower, grass, water and so on). The eye as a function of intentionality and desire selects privileged objects and focuses upon them in an amorous scrutiny. Objects become images and ultimately figures of language. This will be clear from the two texts translated here. Ideally, scrutiny should be maximal and allow the kind of absorption in which the observing ego is sublimated at the expense of the world under observation. The corollary of this in Jaccottet's writing is that the speaking subject should be, again ideally, more of a sensibility than a presence. Jaccottet quotes Simone Weil in this context and the passage carries an ethical weight: 'Whenever we are really attentive, we destroy some of the evil in ourselves... Attentiveness consists in suspending one's thought, leaving it free, empty, so that the object can penetrate through it' (Simone Weil, quoted in *La Semaison*: November 1959). This notion surfaces in various guises throughout Jaccottet's work. A scrutiny that suspends the acquisitions of learning and the details of personal anecdote, by cultivating 'the naked eye', seizes immediacy better. In textual transcription immediacy is, of course, always mediated but the exercise can be viewed as a distrust of pathetic fallacy, as an attempt to let the world speak rather than the ego. Yet the world observed offers insistent and recurrent objects of attention that exceed merely naturalistic description and are transmuted into metaphor by the observer. Nonetheless, Jaccottet regards the claims of self with great caution. Trenchant remarks are reserved for what the French Romantics 'venerated – not without excessive effusion – under the name of *Nature*'. The poet particularly admired by Jaccottet for qualities of "innocent" and "ignorant" response to the natural is Hölderlin. The capacity for this kind of absorption is fallible; it must be seen as an aim not as a permanent achievement. In this light, repetition becomes an important element of scrutiny, particularly for a writer who observes as he walks and moves about. In turn, scrutiny should not be too intense, too keen for the capture, or it will kill its object. Clearly, a great delicacy of observation and, importantly, of transcription is involved.

A further point emerges from this. A landscape, a locality, is of course not merely a series of discrete and static objects but a dynamic pluralism of relationships in movement and therefore in time, time as immediate flux and change, as seasonal iteration and, occasionally in Jaccottet, as history, mainly the past history of a locality or a culture. The privileged figure of these elements in Jaccottet's texts is changing light (and so air and also wind): the play of light through the diurnal and nocturnal cycle, and related to this, changes of colour and seasonal sequence. A whole gamut of *chiaroscuro* is explored, both naturalistically and as metaphorical figure. Titles are indicative here: for instance, *Airs*; *À la lumière d'hiver / Winter light*; *L'Obscurité / Obscurity*. The natural world, then, as a changing 'domain of movement and distances' implies a consciousness of time and mutability and there are various corollaries of this fact that inflect the tonality of Jaccottet's writing and the angle of his inspection.

Moments of fascinated absorption can turn out to be frightening – the sort of fear that ushers in elegy and the long meditation on death and finality which underpins Jaccottet's writing, and is at times foregrounded (in for instance, *À travers un verger / Through an orchard*; *Les Cormorans / Cormorants*; *Leçons / Tenebrae*). Transience is a lyrical commonplace: Jaccottet gives it an idiosyncratic treatment by the minute observation he accords to phenomena of movement. This he calls 'passage' with the word's full semantic resonance, extending from flux to death. Rilke (another important travelling companion) captures the dark side of landscape succinctly in *Worpswede*; 'Alone with the dead, one is not nearly so defenceless as when alone with trees'. The objects, the seasonal patterns and the larger cycles of the natural world are not coterminous with human ones; there are disparities and therefore disquiets. Seasonal iteration can reassure, but it can also underline human finality and fragility. 'Et in Arcadia ego'. Landscape can appear ordinary and familiar, but also alien, full of uneasy distances, a foreign language. But it is a language in the sense that Jaccottet can "transliterate" it, and it can perhaps be learned, even if the recurring question 'What is a place?' (with all its ontological implications) cannot ultimately be answered.

Landscape, then, is the fundamental stimulus to writing for Jaccottet. In fact it becomes a model used in any sort of interpretation, a way of conceiving the world. Jaccottet writes, for instance, of both music and painting with a descriptive technique that translates both arts into topographies. A Rembrandt portrait is discussed in terms of the play of light on a mountain, Schubert chamber music in terms of a the relative distances in a landscape, a Mozart concerto as an interstellar expanse. Landscape also acts as a fundamental model for the verbal text. The text becomes a particular kind of 'landscape' itself, or can be construed in such terms. Jean-Pierre Richard's recent textual analyses, *Pages paysages*, which develop the idea of the page as a landscape, are a helpful critical adjunct to reading Jaccottet in this respect. Jaccottet himself implies that transcription of place is the adjusting of one grammar to another and his writing is full of images of this: wind on water as 'a fugitive inscription on the pages of the earth', darkness as 'thin and threatening ink', the flight of birds as 'calligraphy in the sky'. The whole of the natural scene delivers 'a spoken word', 'a text murmured in a foreign language'. Writing involves translation. It will also need to take heed of movement and flux, and develop a syntax for the moving eye and the ambulatory body.

As I have said, the frequentation of landscapes brings rewarding absorptions but also disquiets. As a writer unconvinced by any form of dogma other than the immediacy of experience, Jaccottet pursues his enquiries in the context of this lack of credo. Fascination with, and scrutiny of natural phenomena are set within the wider and uneasy evidences of the precarious and threatened condition of human experience – a "decentred" world of dislocations and dispersions: 'insecurity, anguish and a marginal sense of life', 'the century that can no longer be stared in the face'. If his work is anchored in a specific locality, this is partly a response to the extreme dispersion of modern living rather than an escape into idyll, though idyll does have a place and is celebrated – sparingly – in his writing. Scattered fragments of an Eden punctuate an otherwise precarious sense of being and they are tenacious, an 'irresistible nostalgia'. Poetic enquiry is marginalised by modern life and Jaccottet's view of the poet as essentially solitary also estimates the claims of poetry as slender. He shares René Char's view of the poet as 'Magicien de l'insécurité' / 'a magician of insecurity'. The visual fascination which promotes the need to write is grounded in doubt and quickened by a sense of finality ('All poetry is the voice given to death'; 'Uncertainty is the motive force, shadow is the source'), and this informs in turn the view of poetry as hesitant enquiry, as a perpetual question, as a means of 'opening doors' to very provisional answers:

> ...cette façon de poser la question qui se nomme la poésie...une manière de parler du monde qui n'explique pas le monde, car ce serait le figer et l'anéantir, mais qui le montre tout nourri de son refus de répondre, vivant parce qu'impénétrable, merveilleux parce que terrible...

> ...poetry, that manner of asking questions...a way of speaking of the world without explaining the world, for that would be to freeze and annihilate it, but showing it nourished by its own refusal to reply, alive because impenetrable, marvellous because terrible...

> (*Éléments d'un songe / Fragments of a dream*)

As a reflection of this 'perpetual question' Jaccottet's writing favours an interrogative mode and adopts various strategies of open-endedness. There is a syntax of the provisional rather than the affirmative: reiteration tries to coax out possible meanings; major statements are relegated to parentheses; conditional tenses attenuate assurances; and there is a whole repertory of the approximative (tentative simile, a rhetoric of 'almost', 'as if ' and so on) in the transcription of an elusive reality. But unlike many contemporary francophone poets, Jaccottet does not bring this sense of questioning hesitancy to bear on the ability of words to convey adequate meaning. One of the deleterious inheritances of Mallarmé's dictum that poetry is born from 'le défaut des langues', the deficiency inherent in existing languages, has been an overly self-reflexive linguistic practice that has constipated much poetry with conceptually orientated preoccupations, and has locked the poem in cerebration at the expense of the expressive resources of the range of non-conceptual functions that link poetic language to music. For Jaccottet, poetry must 'breathe' and while he is by no means unaware of the problematics of signification and reference, his own practice relies more on the resources of poetic syntax than it does on conceptualism, 'the cerebral labyrinth from which one merely emerges in a mutilated state'.

If the world does not reply to the questions asked of it, it nonetheless suggests replies and possibilities, and the development of Jaccottet's rhetoric can be seen as an attempt to centre upon enigma, to approach it as nearly as possible in the hope of grasping its elusive message. Like Bonnefoy, he sees poetry as a form of 'hope', the hope of a world redeemed by close attention to its messages. He has produced a whole body of formal verse and a diversity of texts in prose notable for their range of rhythmic pulse, meticulously concentrated observation, 'sensuous exactness' and a discretion in the voice of the speaking subject which avoids the orotund in favour of self-effacement. His diction moves towards the rhythms of common speech without losing sight of formal patterning.

The elusive encounter with the visible world is most intensely apprehended, in certain texts, as a sense of near epiphany. Elements of landscape and the perceptual and affective response they provoke converge together in a sense of appropriate *mesure* (all the senses of the word need to be mobilised here: proportion, moderation, rhythmical and metrical pulse). Jaccottet calls this convergence a 'centre' and it is described in terms of the transcendence of binary oppositions:

> Toute l'activité poétique se voue à concilier, ou du moins à rapprocher, la limite et l'illimité, le clair et l'obscur, le souffle et la forme. C'est pourquoi le poème nous ramène à notre centre, à notre souci central, à une question métaphysique.

> All poetic activity devotes itself to conciliating or at least to bringing nearer the limited and the limitless, light and darkness, breath and form. This is why the poem returns us to the centre of our being, our central concern, a metaphysical question.

> (*La Semaison:* March 1960)

Sensitive to the excesses of vatic hyperbole, Jaccottet stresses at the same time that this 'centre' arises from the most 'ordinary' and unassuming activity:

...je n'ai fait que passer, accueillir. J'ai vu ces choses, qui elles-mêmes, plus vite ou au contraire plus lentement qu'une vie d'homme, passent. Quelquefois, comme au croisement de nos mouvements (ainsi qu'à la rencontre de deux regards il peut se produire un éclair, et s'ouvrir un autre monde), il m'a semblé deviner, faut-il dire l'immobile foyer de tout mouvement? Ou est-ce déjà trop dire? Autant se remettre en chemin...

I have merely passed by, open to impressions. I have seen those things which also pass – more quickly or, conversely, more slowly than human life. Occasionally, as if our movements had crossed – like the encounter of two glances that can create a flash of illumination and open up another world – I have thought I had glimpsed what I should have to call the still centre of the moving world. Too much said? Better to move on...

(*Paysages avec figures absentes*)

The enigmatic nature of this sort of experience eludes a language of denotation. Its articulation calls for a language of indirection, for the resources of the poem or of lyrical prose.

The poem originates in the sense of 'measure', a 'muted pulse' only perceived in moments of 'great inner stillness' for which it seeks to find equivalence in terms of appropriate rhythm, image and phoneme. Like the experience in which it originates, the poem in turn aims to be a concentrated 'centre' of language. Particular mediations of perception and affect converge in an intensified and unusual linguistic relationship. Here for instance, in a relatively simple example, a convergence of images from the human and the natural cycles (tears and the spring thaw) poignantly encapsulate a parallel and a difference:

Une semaison de larmes	A seedtime of tears
sur le visage changé,	on the changing face,
la scintillante saison	the glistening season
des rivières dérangées:	of rivers in spate:
chagrin qui creuse la terre	grief furrowing the earth
L'âge regarde la neige	Old age watching the snows
s'éloigner sur les montagnes	disappear on the hills

This poem is in Jaccottet's most compressed style and comes, like the first poem I looked at in this introduction, from the atypical collection of haiku-like verse, *Airs*. (Read with the first of the 'Three fantasy pieces' from *Beauregard* it points us to the respective resources of his verse and prose on a similar theme.) Although the minimal style of *Airs* is only one facet of his very varied prosodic and syntactical repertory, it would nonetheless be true to say that Jaccottet regards his verse pieces as the most 'condensed' and privileged form of his writing, and as the form which most nearly approximates to his sense of enigma at its most intensely apprehended, not least because prosody instigates a punctually demanding contract with the reader. But poems, as he points out, like the heightened emotion that occasions them, do not happen every day and he is equally concerned to situate these instances of intensity in the context of contingent life.

For this reason, there is an important relation between the verse and the different forms of prose in Jaccottet's corpus. Poetry is described as a particular and concentrated form of 'breath' ('souffle') and the choice of term, while it centralises the importance of poetry by relating it to breathing as the essential life-sustaining function of the human body, is also a demotion of hyperbolic notions of inspiration. Breathing has its varying intensities and its discontinuities, its different pulses and to these correspond the various pulses of writing, from the prose fragment to the dense resources of the poem. The poem creates a space for 'breathing' to slow down, to concentrate itself and to celebrate its function, prose takes it more for granted. Jaccottet's prose does not merely 'escort' the verse (as the critic Jean Starobinski puts it), it can be read in a fundamental dynamic relation with it. If the poem, not unlike a piece of music, creates its own sense of time, its own dimension outside chronometric time, and is, as Jaccottet has it, a 'suspense' of common language, then prose is related to a more contingent sense of duration, a state of language of a more ordinary kind from which the poem nonetheless springs. The poem is a 'vibrant, mutely sonorous suspense', an intensified moment of language involving more processes of selection and elimination than the more discursive medium of prose. This said, we need to nuance the poetry/prose relationship very carefully indeed in reading Jaccottet's work: some prose pieces are clearly, to use a vexatious term, "prose poems", others, at the opposite end of the spectrum, are fragmented notes. The recent appearance of a volume intercalating verse and prose, *Cahier de verdure / Green notebook* (1990) suggests that the verse/prose dialogue is an important figure in itself.

It is part of Jaccottet's concern that poetry should have a 'place' in a quotidian world of contingencies, however modest a one. His poems are seldom monuments of an exclusive language existing in splendid isolation: he is too conscious of precariousness not to see the poem as an extremely vulnerable object. He has largely managed to disengage his practice from resonances of the French rhetorical tradition and move it towards modest utterance. For Jaccottet ornament should be discreet. So one of the functions of prose in his writing is to provide a broader context for the dense nexus of experience that a poem embodies. Ungaretti, whom he deeply admires, conceived of his whole poetic corpus as one entity, *Vita d'un uomo / The Life of a Man*, and given the particular interdependencies that characterise its range of forms, Jaccottet's work can be seen in similar terms. The question has even broader implications:

> Le livre idéal n'est pas le recueil de poèmes; il n'en comporterait qu'à ses moments les plus purs, comme des fêtes dans l'année verbale...Mais le livre idéal se compose, en fait, de plusieurs livres d'auteurs différents, chacun n'en pouvant réaliser que certains aspects, n'en écrire que certaines pages.

> The ideal book is not the collection of poems; it would only include poems at its purest points, like festivals in a yearly cycle of words...But the ideal book is in fact several books, by different authors, each one capable of dealing only with certain aspects, writing only certain pages.

> (*La Semaison:* October 1966)

Intratext (the network of cross relations within a given author's corpus) broadens here to embrace intertextual dialogue with other writing – a particularly rich feature of Jaccottet's work, though manipulated with a discretion that wears its learning lightly.

The decantation of intense feeling articulated in the given set of relationships between image, rhythm, syntax and phonic patterning in a poem makes it a privileged centre of language, a 'world within world'. It is axiomatic that the image has an important function in this context. Yet Jaccottet, like many of his contemporaries, is distrustful of images. His attitude is ambivalent. The aftermath of Surrealist hegemony, and some would say abuse in this area (too many arbitrary and self-indulgent images amounting in some cases to a whole masturbation fantasy) is marked, in the practice of certain poets, by an austerity and a caution in regard to the image. The rigorously selected images in Jaccottet's verse (less so in his prose where he exploits a more leisurely and contingent mental continuum) are certainly central, but they represent only part of experiential reality: 'in the end all truth is contained for me in an image...', but at the same time '...it is not possible to rely entirely upon images'. Clearly analogy and image-making are an integral part of mental activity, but to become intoxicated with analogy as much of Surrealist practice did is, for Jaccottet, to drift away from evidences of the tangible. To write uniquely in a manner that privileged the image would be to risk setting exquisite pieces in a showcase at the expense of the often sombre background against which they occur:

20

J'imagine qu'un écrivain, saisi...de doute quant à la réalité des issues que ses images les plus pures semblaient lui désigner, puisse...entreprendre de leur trouver leur juste place dans le cours de sa vie (et donc dans la trame de son texte), et de les garder là, lointaines, menacées, précaires, à l'intérieur d'un ensemble plus rude et plus opaque; pour éviter de les "monter en épingle", c'est-à-dire de les figer, de les dénaturer.

I imagine that a writer...who is gripped with doubt about the reality of the solutions his purest images seemed to point out it him, might...undertake to situate them appropriately in the context of his life (and thereby in the main thread of his text) and to keep them there, at a distance, threatened, precarious, within a rougher, less distinct pattern of the whole, so as to avoid "mounting them for display", that is, making them stagnant and unnatural.

(*À travers un verger* / *Through an orchard*)

These remarks can be extended to the balance between prose and verse in Jaccottet's work as a whole. By relating the concentrated moments/worlds represented by his poems to an extensive and various body of prose writing, he avoids the party-piece of the "achieved" poem, and provides an intratext which invites us into (or alternatively out of) the 'suspended' and more enigmatic language of the poems. The most obvious instance of this is *La Semaison* and the other lyrical diary/notebooks which he has been publishing regularly since 1963. The same is true of the many critical essays and reviews he has published, notably those collected in *L'Entretien des muses* / *The Parley of the Muses* and in *Une Transaction secrète* / *A Secret undertaking*.

Very occasionally his prose texts (I am thinking particularly of 'Travaux au lieu dit l'étang' in *Paysages avec figures absentes*) actually plot the process from observed phenomenon to poem, and some are clearly 'pre-texts' for the poem. This is a further gesture towards poetic "democracy", and here the practice of Francis Ponge, about whom Jaccottet has written briefly but with deft pertinence, was encouraging. Ponge's *La Rage de l'expression* / *The Mania to express* was obviously important in opening (or pretending to open) the writer's work-desk up to the reader, with all that implied about poetry as a form of daily work rather than the subjective and 'flabby lyricism' Ponge found so repulsive in a long Romantic tradition. Phenomenology offered a corrective and a reorientation for poetry. Ponge's scrutiny of ordinary objects and his insistence on 'le-regard-de-telle-sorte-qu'on-le-parle' / 'the to-be-spoken gaze' are also relevant elements of Jaccottet's orientation. Jaccottet does not adopt Ponge's onomastics or exploit the same historical sense of language implicit in his etymologies; his own eye is more inclined to 'singing' than to just 'speaking', but he does share the salutory conviction that poetry is an integral part of the everyday, 'a modest attention to limited things' and that making it accessible matters. Prose has an important function to play here. The two collections we have translated in this volume will exemplify this and it is time to turn to them.

III. *Beauregard*

Beauregard (1981) is a collection of prose pieces analogous in Jaccottet's output to prose collections like *La Promenade sous les arbres / Walking beneath trees* and P*aysages avec figures absentes*. Yet in formal terms it is more homogeneous than these earlier collections in which lyrical and discursive prose rub shoulders, polarising or combining with less sense of formal unity. These earlier prose collections have much to say about Jaccottet's writing practice. In *Beauregard* this is implicit and less obtrusive. The work is a collection of 'landscapes in prose' (*paysages* is given this sense in *La Semaison*), place reassembled as text, a mode of writing which Jaccottet developed early in his career and which he has made distinctively his own and brought to a high point of expressive achievement. *Beauregard* was written almost concurrently with *Pensées sous les nuages* and there are many echoes between the two works, as there had been between *La Promenade sous les arbres* and *L'Ignorant / In Ignorance*, and between *Paysages avec figures absentes* and *Airs*. But it would be misleading to suggest that the prose collections are paraphrases of the verse ones. As I have said, prose and formal verse have a subtler dialogue than this in Jaccottet's work. The exploitation of intratext in his writing is part of a general strategy of reiteration, a means of lingering on some of his major preoccupations, presenting them in a variety of mediations, a contrapuntal performance which can be seen as musical in conception. The constant sense of echo between one work and another, as well as the thematic recurrences, plot a patient investigation of an uncertain world and also offer the reader a series of helpful parallels for construing it.

None of this is to suggest that the individual collections (verse and prose) lack autonomy and distinctiveness. They are simply not "closed" texts in the final analysis. *Beauregard* has a unity of its own and can be easily read as an autonomous piece of writing. The texts that constitute it are characteristic of Jaccottet's *paysages*: in them the eye is invariably arrested by some striking stimulus which provokes a subsequent meditation. I use meditation here very much in the sense given it by Louis Martz in his classic work *The Poetry of Meditation*:

> ...a meditative poem is a work that creates an interior drama of the mind; this dramatic action...is usually created by some form of self-address, in which the mind grasps firmly a problem or situation deliberately evoked by the memory, brings it forward toward the full light of consciousness and concludes with a moment of illumination, where the speaker's self has, for a time, found an answer to its conflicts.

Likewise, the meditative patterns in *Beauregard* are structured towards a tentative "resolution": they give the impression of moving towards the possibility of a poem and this is signalled by the often condensed and metaphorical final paragraphs. In some of Jaccottet's *paysages* antecedent to *Beauregard* there is occasionally an over self-conscious manipulation of this process at work, a slight fussiness of manner. Here the prose is more self-assured (notably in the ease of its play with images) and less self-conscious. At the same time it is highly organised. The five pieces are carefully patterned and balanced, although, typically, expressions of approximation and the frequency of the interrogative mode do not draw attention to the fact.

There is an obvious external patterning to these five texts in the sense that they are arranged, like many of Jaccottet's works, in a seasonal sequence that moves from winter ('Beauregard') to late summer or early autumn ('Starlings'). Against this cycle of seasonal time, the time of human life is implicitly measured with a quite characteristic sense of disquiet, urgency and elegy in a muted use of the literary commonplace, the *carpe diem* topos (and sometimes a *memento mori*): '...accept all this...before you are cast to the ground' ('April'). 'All this' is presumably the profusion of the landscape, although it is interesting also that landscape often provokes an erotic response (in 'March' and at the end of 'Starlings' particularly) which heightens the *carpe diem* topos even more dramatically. 'Seasonal' structure is a clear signal of the patterning. Another, less immediately obvious patterning, and it is characteristic not only of Jaccottet but of contemporaries like André du Bouchet and Yves Bonnefoy, is the recurring preoccupation with the four elements: 'Beauregard' plays predominantly on fire, 'March' on water, 'April' on earth, 'May' on air and light, 'Starlings' on air. In all five texts Jaccottet's central thematics of light is ubiquitous.

Within these broad patterns, each text is itself carefully structured: cleverly and unobtrusively so, since the impression transmitted on a first reading suggests a leisured and fairly spontaneous procedure.

'Beauregard', the first of the five pieces, describes a striking locality that acts as a gateway to the magic of desiring fantasy: the 'other side' of the mountain, the 'passage beyond', a recurrent figure in his work. This is not allowed to flood the text and is held in check by a use of ironic deflation. In a sense, the irony serves to give the fantasy more credibility so that it becomes only partially illusory. The description hovers, typically, between the physical facts of place and an 'interior landscape'. This is no doubt endemic in the whole business of inscribing landscape in the referential system of words, moving from a visual to a verbal semiosis. The descriptive technique is so deft that the transition is barely noticeable and here Jaccottet has absorbed his lessons from Rilke rather than from a writer in the French tradition such as Baudelaire. After a meticulous description of a locality and the imaginative fantasy provoked by it, the text is ordered around the resonances of a name (like the imaginative excursions of Proust's 'Nom de pays: le nom' – the final section of *Du côté de chez Swann / Swann's Way*). In 'Beauregard' the excursions are predominantly mnemonic (a return to a childhood locality of the same name) and intertextual – with a reference to a poem by Montale with the place name Beauregard (Bellosguardo) in its title. The pattern moves from recorded fact, through fantasy and childhood memory, to the memory of another text, associated in turn with a memory of Italy. The predominant element is fire: the fire of village lamplight, of the quarry, of the 'glazed earthenware stoves' of childhood, of the warm glow of Italy – the first line of the Montale poem is 'nella corusca distesa' / 'in the glowing stretch'. The 'fire' is – characteristically – threatened by 'dark' and 'cold' and the text ends with a sombre reflection on finalities in a coda that will become increasingly less grave as the collection proceeds.

'March', with its extended central image of melting snows as hair unpinned and falling free, polarises between the distant summit of a mountain and the landscape that extends beneath it, and becomes an emblematic setting for the contrasting cycles of human and natural experience. The choice of the central image also conveys the erotic fascination that the scene arouses and that in turn is set in the optic of approaching old age prone to nostalgia. Nostalgia is countered cleverly by an exploitation of visual delight as a cleansing blessing, a continually present stimulus to the eye, even a frail promise of transcending finalities. Finally the scene recorded is condensed into a paradoxical and allusive formulation, again tempered with irony: the snows become a coin (an obol, another recurring image) to be kept for Charon, ensuring a 'safe passage' to death, but in the absence of any assured mythology: 'Je garderai cette obole blanche pour le passeur qu'il n'y a plus' / 'I shall keep this white obol for the boatman who is no longer part of our world'. This problematic mythology of death and gods will be taken up in 'May'.

'April', placed significantly at the centre of the collection, uses an image that figures somewhat less prominently in Jaccottet's other works: the poet-gardener. The image is developed here to present an unobtrusive and persuasively understated *art poétique*. It is a formulation of Jaccottet's view of the scope and function of poetry and its ordinariness and utter modesty distance his project from any inflated claim for writing. Elsewhere he uses the related idea of poems (and writing generally) as mere seeds tossed by the wind, germinating only on suitable ground. Common ground. In 'April' there is the further image of the poet as would-be herbalist/doctor, a succinct reminder that poems are 'infusions' of language ('decantations' is the word he uses elsewhere): they come about through 'slow infiltration'. They hold the possibilities of cure.

'May', specifically related intratextually to 'Le pré de mai' / 'The May meadow' in *Paysages avec figures absentes*, revisits the difficulty of adequately translating the sense of place in a moment of suspense between daylight and nightfall. Dusk, together with dawn, is one of Jaccottet's elective motifs, a moment suspended 'between two worlds' which defeats binary oppositions. Hesitations of light often usher in uncertainty of mood and the speculations here revolve around the vulnerability of poetry in a demythologised sense of history in which gods are absent. Jaccottet's affinities with Hölderlin and his high estimation of Greek culture are implicit in these metaphysical reflections. The subject is dismissed only to return at the end of the text in the notion of poetry as prayer in a godless world. The text is structured this time around two colours, the silver of eve-ning light and the green of darkening meadow grass and vegetation. These colours return the text to the persistence of the natural cycle and make a virtue of the available landscape in the absence of other reassurances.

The final text of the collection, 'Starlings', is unified by the image of a festival, which the text tries to undermine ironically in a parenthesis, suggesting that writing of this kind is a clumsy conjuring trick. The sense of dynamic energy in this piece is quite remarkable and the writing virtuoso, particularly in the syntax and the 'stunning' imagery of electrification, arrows and fireworks deployed to convey the speed, suddenness and sound of a bizarre spectacle. It is typical of Jaccottet's declared commitment to self-effacement and understatement that anything that risks flamboyancy should be ironically dismissed. But here, the attempt at dismissal and self-denigration in the parenthesis only serves to draw attention to the virtuosity of the writing. And perhaps deliberately: Jaccottet knows enough about rhetoric to realise the potential of the false modesty topos in literature.

The five texts of *Beauregard* are, then, carefully contrived but unobtrusively so. The title of the three central sections, 'Three fantasy pieces', has a certain appropriateness to the texture of the writing as a whole: Jaccottet allows himself a freer rein in *Beauregard*, particularly in relation to the adventitious image, than he does in earlier prose texts where there are constant riders about the danger of imagery as distracting from reality. The licence implied by the word 'fantasy' (including its connotations of 'triviality' in French) is certainly evident in the free play of metaphor and association but, at the same time, and bearing in mind the musical significance of the word *fantasia*, this freedom does not preclude a control of the formal motifs structuring the writing. Immediacy and patterning are balanced with nicety and the hesitation between them gives *Beauregard* a distinctive place in Jaccottet's prose.

All five texts are initially motivated by some arresting visual focus of an apparently literal, almost naturalistic kind, which is then followed through in a pattern of meditation that exceeds the visually literal, the merely optical: associations in memory, intertext, transpositions into other orders of sense experience. This is particularly true of sound: Jaccottet "looks" as much with the ear as with the eye – 'l'œil écoute'/ 'the eye listens' in Claudel's words. For instance, the raked patterns of the soil in 'April' become 'the vibrations of a voice, the notation of a song…a song from silent lips'. The associative movements of these texts seek to plot the elusive "speech" of landscape, to relate its various elements together to a point where the process of writing a poem seems imminent. The texts tend to close with a more enigmatic and compressed formulation that relates back to their preceding pages, but seems ready to take off in a new direction of language. Jaccottet has frequently described certain of his prose texts as patient journeys towards the poem. In *Beauregard* that suggestion certainly exists, but implicitly enough to allow the texts to stand on their own. If on the one hand the language reads in a leisured manner, rhythmed by cleverly nuanced reiterative patterns and hesitating between various possibilities of articulation, on the other, it organises itself quite clearly at times, as Andrea Cady's work has shown, into balanced syllabic and syntactic patterns, phonic and rhythmic repetitions, strongly suggestive of verse prosody. It has not really been possible to "translate" these: the nearest approximations possible have been offered.

The texts of *Beauregard* convey admirably the way a particular scrutiny of and response to the visual world translate into language directed towards the possibility of a poem. This is signalled from the start. Already in the final section of the eponymous text the word '*Beauregard*' itself has been translated into Italian, the 'Bellosguardo' of the Montale poem (from *Le Occasioni*): this is emblematic of a whole verbal semiotics of translation from the seen to the unseen, from the village of *Beauregard* and its setting to the fantasies and memories it provokes. They are provoked as much by the sound of the word itself – *Beauregard* – as by the sense of sight. Visual and the verbal converge in a place name. By transposing the word into Italian it is rendered "strange", "other": beauregard > bellosguardo. Semantics have not in fact altered (in both languages the word means 'beautiful sight') but the 'colouring' of the word has, just as the literally visual, the naturalistic description at the beginning of the text is affectively transformed by the inner eye of memory and fantasy. Nothing is merely optical, and in a Jaccottet text nothing is merely literal. But the Italian word just happens, of course, to be associated with a poem, a poem which is "entered into" at the end of the text through memories of Italy, of Florence and of a balcony in Florence in particular. In Montale's elegiac poem, 'Tempi di Bellosguardo', the meditation is conducted from an eminence above Florence, and this provokes, in the Jaccottet text, a memory of a view down from a hotel balcony in the same city. Jaccottet concludes 'Beauregard' by extending the implications of the word a stage further, this time to the eyes, the beautiful gaze (*le beau regard*) in the eyes of the woman standing beside the subject on the balcony. Finally, and again very much in the same sort of resonance as the Montale poem, there is emphasis on the loveliness of the seen and the named which Jaccottet's text has so richly explored, but also a sombre reminder that eyes eventually close forever, that sight is finite (or is it?), and that no 'magic of words' can obviate this. The rich exploitation of the visual here takes us well beyond any naive sense of the picturesque: it depends on meticulously controlled language, acuteness of both the optical and the "inner" eye, and deft manipulation of intertextual possibility.

The way the mediations between the visible and the verbal, sight and sound are explored in this initial text and in *Beauregard* as a whole, make it a particularly rich introduction to the more concentrated texture of Jaccottet's verse, not least because it hovers constantly on that threshold. A poem from *Airs* equates song and sight thus:

> Qu'est-ce donc que le chant?   What then is song?
> Rien qu'une sorte de regard   Merely a way of looking

What this 'mere looking' implies, *Beauregard* amply enacts. I turn next to *Under Clouded Skies*, the verse collection written during the same period.

IV. *Pensées sous les nuages / Under Clouded Skies*

Most of this collection was written in 1982–83, with the first two parts dating from 1976. So it is a near contemporary of *Beauregard*. The thematic echoes between the two collections have already been mentioned and they will be obvious to any reader.

Pensées sous les nuages is a particularly rewarding introduction to Jaccottet's verse because it relates back to an already considerable body of poetry and represents a mature culmination of the various formal, thematic and tonal features of earlier collections. A whole body of already accomplished verse precedes it. There is nothing unfamiliar thematically but the broad characteristic that distinguishes this collection from others is what I can only call an ease of performance. Jaccottet had aimed from early on to achieve an equilibrium of the conversational and the formal, 'un ton, un rythme, un accent, une façon de maintenir le discours à mi-hauteur entre la conversation et l'éloquence' / 'a tone, a rhythm, an accent, a means of keeping speech poised half way between the conversational and the formally eloquent' (*La Promenade sous les arbres*). The flexible prosody and the characteristic lexis deployed to this end in *Pensées sous les nuages* is more various than in any previous single collection of verse.

Since *Beauregard* and *Pensées sous les nuages* have very obvious connections thematically, I shall not linger on each individual piece as I did in the previous section. Where there is new thematic material, I shall comment. But what I say here is principally animated by consideration of what is involved in reading Jaccottet's verse. Verse is arguably more open-ended than prose – it is in this case – and I also have to admit to a distrust of interpreting the individual poem for the reader. In broad terms, verse, like music, is less semantically stable than prose and its real life is contained in the contract that each reader makes with it. So I am more concerned in this section with matters of approach than with interpretations. Where there are possible problems in the reading, I have tried to indicate them. Before turning directly to *Pensées sous les nuages*, some general review of Jaccottet's notion of the verse poem seems appropriate.

If prose writing is particularly suitable, as Jaccottet sees it, for the contingent world and its accidents of time and space, following the leisurely rhythms and adventitious thoughts of the walker/traveller who figures so prominently in his work, then verse poetry is by contrast something altogether more concentrated, 'decanted', as I said earlier. It is a peak of verbal expression, with a different relation to the contingent world, temporally less naturalistic and less linear. The elements of narration become minimal. The very physical appearance of verse on the page already signals a reading that is less (or differently) sequential than that suggested by blocks of prose text. Because it embodies features such as rhyme and phonic patterning, rhythm and the phrasal articulation implied by its lineation, we are led to draw analogies with music and musical performance.

Jaccottet has had a good deal to say on the language of poetry. An early expression of ambitions reads as follows:

> Rêve d'écrire un poème qui serait aussi cristallin et aussi vivant qu'une oeuvre musicale, enchantement pur, mais non froid...une musique de paroles communes, rehaussée peut-être ici et là d'une appoggiature, d'un trille limpide.

> To be able to write a poem as crystalline and alive as a piece of music, pure enchantment, but not cold abstraction...a music of common words, possibly embellished in places with an appogiatura or a clear trill.

(*La Semaison:* January 1959)

The limpidity of music finds an equivalence in common speech, its living quality in rhyme, in phonic patterning, but above all in rhythm and pulse. These "musical" matters are notoriously difficult to write about in relation to a verbal art but some insistence is necessary here because the musical analogy is a frequent reference point in Jaccottet's work. He can, for instance, even imagine landscape as 'une œuvre musicale qui se serait immobilisée devant nous avec tous ses rapports, ses silences et ses accents' / 'a piece of music immobilised before our eyes with all its interrelations, rests and accentuation' (*La Promenade sous les arbres*). But more relevantly, poetry, the 'murmur' apprehended in moments of great inner stillness, is described as a pulse or measure ('une mesure', as I suggested earlier, means musical beat, but also a sense of proportion), as a variable 'breath' that it is the business of verse to render, and render as naturally as possible in language at once accessible and strange. To this end, rhythmic pulse needs to be apparent enough to register a departure from the rhythms of common speech without calling attention to the fact:

>...un rythme, volontaire mais plus ou moins soumis à des règles con-
ventionnelles, rythme dont le principal effet est sans doute de dégager
immédiatement le texte de tout souci d'utilité afin qu'il flotte dans l'air
un peu au-dessus de l'utile mais pas trop au-dessus pour ne pas perdre
contact avec l'espèce de réalité au sein de laquelle vivent les hommes.
La poésie devient alors simple nomination des choses, et rejoint, sans
pour autant se confondre avec elle, une certaine forme de prière.

>...a rhythm with a will of its own but governed by conventional rules
to a greater or lesser extent; a rhythm whose chief effect is perhaps to
disengage the text from any preoccupation with functional practicality so
that it hovers a little above that but not so much so that it loses contact
with the kind of world in which we live. Poetry in this sense becomes
a simple naming of things and relates to a certain form of prayer but
without identifying itself with prayer.

>(*La Promenade sous les arbres*)

Musical elements are clearly important. What is also important is
the emphasis on the 'ordinariness' of the enterprise: nothing should
be too formal, too self-consciously worked. This discretion in the
'musical' side of poetic craft is paralleled in the development of
Jaccottet's choice of forms: he moves away from the relatively fixed
forms of the early verse towards an asymetrical prosody, nearer to
natural speech rhythms, controlled at the same time by a masterly
sense of lineation and a constant ability to make the ghost of met-
rical regularity somehow present (at times explicitly) amid the irr-
egular verse. These remarks are central to Jaccottet's distinctive
prosody and in almost every one of his collections of verse, whether
it be the minimalist manner of *Airs* or the 'discursive' and more
ample syntax of a collection like *À la lumière d'hiver.*

Antecedent to *Pensées sous les nuages,* the collections of verse, at
least those that come after *L'Effraie / The Screech Owl* and *L'Ignorant,*
which established his reputation as a poet, tend to polarise: on the
one hand, short, compressed styles with rigorously selective imagery,
lyric understatement and a certain amount of ellipsis and parataxis
(syntax that functions through juxtaposition of clauses not connected
by conjunctions); at the other end of the scale, more ample lineation,
hypotaxis (syntax relying on subordinate clauses with co-ordinating
conjunctions), more explicit poetic argument and, in the collections
after *Leçons*, freer imagery and lyrical sweep. These two polarities
(once again I oversimplify for the sake of clarity and the opposition,
like that between verse and prose, needs to be nuanced) are sketched
in an early note in the following terms:

>Sans doute le poème en vers longs et réguliers suppose-t-il un souffle
assez ample et paisible...Solennisation des choses, des instants, accord,
harmonie, bonheur...Il y a une difficulté intéressante dans l'opposition

entre le poème-instant (celui de l'*Allegria* d'Ungaretti) et le poème-discours...tel un bref récit légèrement solennel, psalmodié à deux doigts au-dessus de la terre.

Perhaps a poem with long regular lines indicates a rather deep and calm breathing pattern...the ceremonial celebration of things, of moments, acceptance, harmony, happiness...There is an interesting problem in the opposition between the poem of the moment (like those of Ungaretti in *L'Allegria*) and the "discursive" poem, the poem that is like a brief account of something, slightly solemn, chanted a hair's breadth above the earth.

(*La Semaison:* March 1960)

By the time of *Pensées sous les nuages* this sort of polarisation has been absorbed into a broader prosodic and stylistic practice which embraces whatever particular form is appropriate. So the short poem of convergent sensations, taken to its extreme in *Airs* where the poem is very often a deixis – literally so, 'un simple doigt tendu' / 'simply a finger pointing' – lies behind the poems of 'On voit' / 'Things seen', those in the Purcell sequence and many of the poem/fragments in 'Le mot joie' / 'The Word Joy'. The aim of the concentrated, short poem is perhaps best stated in *Paysages avec figures absentes* and I quote the passage here as a helpful reading aid. It comes from a piece called 'Si les fleurs n'étaient que belles...' / 'If flowers were merely beautiful...', important for understanding Jaccottet's notion of poetry and place, and occurs after the insertion of a short poem in the style of *Airs*:

Voilà ce qu'il arrive qu'un poème essaie de saisir, en peu de mots. Non pas une histoire, ni un drame, ni une réflexion que le temps, un temps plus ou moins long, mesure; mais la coïncidence, ou du moins la convergence, à demi confuse, de plusieurs sensations qu'une analyse stériliserait.

This is what a poem sometimes tries to seize upon, in few words. Not a narrative, not a drama, nor a reflexion measured out more or less extensively in time, but the coincidence, or at least the convergence of several sensations which analysis would make sterile.

The very fact that this passage is followed by an arguably more successful version in lyrical prose of the poem in question points to a disquiet about the autonomy of such short, elliptical poems. Jaccottet's ultimate solution is to develop the syntax of such compressed forms away from parataxis towards a more hypotactic syntax. This is what we find in the short poems in *Pensées sous les nuages* where the syntax is more discursive (that is, it controls the direction of meaning more than the ellipsis of *Airs* which is arguably more ambivalent and semantically pluralistic). This by no means removes the sense of enigma from the short poem (witness the sixth of the 'On voit' sequence for instance); it is conveyed less by elliptical syntax than by a freer use of image. There is also the fact that in *Pensées sous les nuages* the short poems are grouped in sequences under a general title. The effect is to produce an engaging tension between thematic stability and the less stable intermittencies of point of view (temporal, perceptual, affective and so on).

It is clear that short lyrics are an important element of Jaccottet's poetics. Elusive and minimal signs (often connected with instants of virtual epiphany) are in some way the best guarantee of authenticity: 'plus le signe se dérobe, plus il y a de chances qu'il ne soit pas une illusion' / 'the more elusive the sign, the less chance of it being an illusion' (*Paysages avec figures absentes*). Brevity and minimal means also correspond to a sense of the infrequent, vulnerable and tenuous nature of important perceptions and feelings. They confer a sense of the relative importance we might accord to poetic experience in a world which has other and often opposed claims and they point in the direction of fragility and diffidence. There is a paradox of the utterly negligible and the precious. Like Ponge again, Jaccottet, in his concern with 'utterly ordinary' phenomena, points us in the direction of the complexity and wonder of 'simple things'. For both poets, this starts to become manifest as soon as the apparently simple is verbally articulated. 'C'est le tout à fait simple qui est impossible à dire'/ 'It is the utterly simple that is impossible to put into words' (*Paysages avec figures absentes*). Jaccottet sets himself an exacting task here: 'ne rien expliquer, mais prononcer juste' / 'avoid explaining a thing, but find exactly the right words to convey it' (*La Semaison:* November 1959). '*Simple* naming of things'? I have said that for Jaccottet the poem is a privileged world and as such is an exception rather than a rule. Again the short form seems to be a way of conveying this. It demands dense richness but only for a short space. An early (and frequently misquoted) poetic motto for Jaccottet was 'À partir du rien. Là est ma loi' / 'Starting from the least thing. That is my rule' (*La Semaison:* March 1962). This succinctly encapsulates the fragility of his poetic entreprise. The final word on the virtues of minimal and fragile means must go to the liminary poem of *Airs* as the best gloss of this important element of Jaccottet's poetic identity. It summarises many of the points I have made, having as its starting point 'the least thing':

Peu de chose, rien qui chasse	Very little, nothing that banishes
l'effroi de perdre l'espace	the terror of losing our world
est laissé à l'âme errante	is left to the nomad spirit

Mais peut-être, plus légère,	But maybe – less burdened,
incertaine qu'elle dure,	doubtful of its future –
est-elle celle qui chante	it is the spirit that sings
avec la voix la plus pure	most purely
les distances de la terre	the distances of the earth

This frail and tentative celebration of the virtues of travelling lightly in a context of threatened dispossession is a reversal of many poetic myths of confident acquisition, and the intriguing final line, fore-grounding the word 'distances', undermines possible expectations of a cliché like 'the beauties of the earth' and invites us to ponder a range of semantic attributions. The positive or negative force of 'distances' remains undecidable and this keeps the poem utterly alive.

Short poems, in which there is a punctual convergence of elements, cast into what Jaccottet calls 'a secret syntax' which arrests the attention of the reader, demand a more than usual interpretative participation. It is axiomatic that for Jaccottet the world is elusive and ungraspable. More broadly, commentators have emphasised the experience of reality as 'loss' in much contemporary French poetry (and writing generally). What they do not perhaps stress enough is that if the nature of reality is to be construed as loss and elusiveness, then the poem – or a certain sort of poetry – can be an enabling vehicle of enquiry for the construction of elusive perceptions and feelings. A poetic style can choose to be more concerned with approaches than with finalities, and its particular rhetoric can induce an engagement of the attention analogous (and arguably more intense) to acts of attention in the perceptual and affective world of daily experience. 'Presence', to use Yves Bonnefoy's word, can be reconstituted in the act of reading, with the poem as an aid to attentiveness and meditation. In the case of the short Jaccottet poem attentiveness is achieved very often by an exploitation of a convergence of affect and percept caught in a densely compressed nexus of elements: paratactic syntax, phonic recurrence and rhyme, arresting image and metaphor. Such a poem not only makes demands on the reader, but by not underestimating her/him, confers a respect alien to a more "hieratic" style (that of the poet as high priest of a superior ontological status and knowledge, that bogey of so much of the French tradition and still, unfortunately, very much in evidence).

Associated with "hieratic" stances too is the cultivation of obscure and difficult vocabulary. In the wake of Francis Ponge again, Jaccottet, without oversimplifying the intriguing "difficulty" of the simplest language, opts for the most "transparent" words possible. He seeks, as he puts it, 'to speak with the voice of daylight' / 'parler avec la voix du jour' (also translatable as 'the voice on offer' as in 'plat du jour', again an emphasis on the ordinary). Reading his verse, our energies are not mobilised to decode an obscure lexis (frequently the case in Deguy, in Bonnefoy and many others), but to attend to syntax, image and the patterns of a meaning which is governed as much by phonic and rhythmical features as by conceptual ones. These are elements which, in their appeal to the body as well as the mind, aim to connect the reader more directly with a language of 'being', the 'grammar of ontology' that Octavio Paz sees as a fundamental function of poetry.

The short poems of *Pensées sous les nuages* can be read in the light of what I have said above, with the rider that their syntax is less elliptical than that of some of the earlier ones. Their punctuation is also less ambiguous. It is worth mentioning that 'Things seen', 'To Henry Purcell' and 'The Word Joy' are conceived as sequences of short poems not as single ones. In the case of 'The Word Joy', and unusually for Jaccottet who admits to perplexity in the face of the typographical idiosyncracies of a poet like André du Bouchet, the layout is a typographical departure. But not a perplexing one. The spacing of the poems, often floating in isolated fragments on the white of the page, can be construed fairly obviously as the splintered fragments of remembered 'joy' with which the text is concerned and which is glossed in the liminary prose. It amounts to a graphic syntax of the unpredictabilities of memory. The graphic representation also relates to a notion of the ecstatic as elusive and only to be experienced in scattered fragments: as one of the poems states, 'je ne peux plus parler qu'à travers ces fragments' / 'my only way of speaking is through fragments'. The broader issue of the intermittent nature of any apprehension of perfection which figures frequently in Jaccottet's writing is a notion he has related to a famous fragment of Novalis: 'Paradise is dispersed over the whole earth, that is why we do not recognise it. Its scattered features must be reunited'. It is therefore possible to read the fragmented layout of 'The Word Joy' as a kind of spatial syntax which articulates the intermittent nature not only of the poem's central emotion (joy) but of a whole range of intermittent elements: perception, memory and the possibility of the poem itself. The pursuit of the poem, that rarity, is a pursuit conducted through mist: 'Je suis comme quelqu'un qui creuse dans la brume' / 'I am like a man digging in the mist' (and mist becomes another possible interpretation of the blank space in the sequence). The pursuit is nonetheless characteristically persistent and patient:

Mais chaque jour, peut-être, on peut reprendre
le filet déchiré, maille après maille,
et ce serait, dans l'espace plus haut,
comme recoudre, astre à astre, la nuit...

But perhaps every day we can gather up again
the torn net, stitch by stitch,
and it would be, in the higher spaces,
like sewing the night together star by star...

Here, as elsewhere in *Pensées sous les nuages*, the image of the torn net joins a similar one at the end of the second paragraph of 'Starlings' in *Beauregard*.

Brevity of form is by no means ubiquitous in Jaccottet's verse and I turn now to the more extended poems. The fuller-bodied lineation of 'Thoughts under the clouds' and 'Laments for a dead companion' in particular indicate a somewhat different poetic style, that of the discursive poem. What this means has essentially to do with syntax, and poetic argument is conveyed explicitly by the use of hypotaxis. Jaccottet established a 'discursive' poetic manner in *L'Ignorant* and saw this at the time as his distinctive poetic manner, before he became acquainted with Japanese haikai in the 1960s and developed the elliptical and minimalist style of *Airs*. *Airs* was followed by one of the finest of his collections, *Leçons*, a collection of relatively short (but by no means elliptical) poems in which the brevity of form discards the stark juxtapositions and compressed formulations of haiku and returns to discursive syntax. The tenor of Jaccottet's poetry has always been meditative, speculative ('cette façon de poser la question...') so that parataxis must be regarded as uncharacteristic. But the practice of something akin to haiku conferred even more economy upon his poetic style than was apparent earlier. After *Airs* and *Leçons* a much more ample prosody develops with the poems of *Chants d'en bas / Songs from down there* and *À la lumière d'hiver* where the verse is freer and less symmetrical than it was earlier. Jaccottet characterises the collections from *Chants d'en bas* on as a move in the direction of what he calls 'le grand lyrisme', the broad lyric sweep of Hölderlin and the Rilke of the *Duineser Elegien* in particular. Apostrophe, expansive lineation, long and complex sentence structure are characteristic of this. Interesting too in *Pensées sous les nuages* are thematic allusions to Hölderlin and Rilke.

Like *Beauregard*, *Pensées sous les nuages* is anchored in landscape and the reactions provoked by the eye. 'Things seen' and much of 'The Word Joy', the one a series of glimpses, the other a more fragmented and sporadic presentation of the visual, contain much that is common to both collections. But the volume also contains important preoccupations not foregrounded in *Beauregard*: notably death and music.

If the natural world can suggest possibilities of transcendence and illumination, moments of epiphany, there is also its finite and imperfect side, expressed in the long meditation on death, mutability and finality that gives Jaccottet's verse its disquieted and sombre undertow. This is present in the poem 'To a young mother' where the misfortune of an imperfect birth is related to the wider issues of war in the Middle East by an elliptical link conferred by the ambiguity of an antonomastic apostrophe: 'Daughter of Zion' signals Jerusalem as well as the young mother. The poem is unsuccessful in these terms, not only because of the rather tenuous rhetorical device but because it foregrounds domestic tragedy and marginalises the wider issues to which it attempts to allude. More impressively, the threnody, or song of lamentation, for the poet Pierre-Albert Jourdan, 'Laments for a dead Companion', articulates the pathos and the anger of a death with the same impressive force that characterised Jaccottet's finest collection of poetry of mourning, *Leçons*.

Jourdan was a contemporary of Jaccottet and their work has remarkable affinities. Interestingly there is a prose account of the death in *Autres Journées / Further days* (entry for September 1981), a continuation of *La Semaison*. For anyone gripped by the poem, the prose account offers a further gloss on prose / verse transformations. The poem, provoked by the finality of a death and the extremity of physical pain in a terminal illness, uses complex hypotaxis to excellent effect, particularly in the third section where the strangled wish to offer comfort for pain in the form of music (and by implication, poetry) is conveyed by the syntactic tangle, itself implied in the line, 'Vous, lentes voix qui vous nouez et dénouez' / 'Slow voices ravelling and unravelling'. Syntactic 'tangle' is counterpointed in the poem by bald, short statement and, characteristically, by tense and frightened interrogatives. The threnody is conducted, again characteristically, in terms of landscape: a death is envisaged (as it was in *Leçons*) using the metaphor of a journey, and the setting alludes to topographies like Dante's hell and to mythological perils like Scylla and Charybdis ('les rochers rapprochés' / 'the closing walls'). Here, the landscape is more powerfully and dramatically internalised ('dans le ciel intérieur' / 'in the heaven inside') than usual, and we are reminded that landscape can be used when necessary to produce an allegorical discourse:

> On voudrait, pour ce pas qu'il doit franchir
> – si l'on peut parler de franchir
> là où la passerelle semble interrompue

et l'autre rive prise dans la brume
ou elle-même brume, ou pire: abîme –
dans ce vent barbelé,
l'envelopper, meurtri comme il l'est, de musique...

One would like, for the crossing he has to make
– if we can speak of a crossing
when the bridge seems broken off
and the other bank in a mist
or itself a mist, or worse, an abyss –
in this barbed-wire wind
to wrap him in music, hurt as he is...

This passage will serve to illustrate the elements of poetic style I have mentioned. Its careful and discreet phonic patterning (assonance and alliterative recurrence particularly) and the "conversational" speech patterns conferred by its careful lineation will be immediately obvious. The lines use a landscape of a journey to the underworld shrouded in mist, thus exploiting the recurrent figure of the whole collection – mist, cloud, obfuscation, obstacle, limitations to comprehension. With the equivalence mist/abyss, the external elements of landscape become eclipsed and the verse brings us from visual detail to affect (fear and nothingness), before returning to the crossing and the wind which accompanies it. It is a 'barbed-wire wind' which not only enlarges the subject of the individual death to include collective deaths by its resonance of the camps and barbed-wire enclosure, but prefigures the tonality of the final section of the poem which again alludes to interrogation and torture – 'I saw him between two sessions, in a respite: / they had not been gentle with him', and the use of the word 'Commandant' – images translating the pain of terminal illness (Jourdan died of cancer) but again broadening the subject from individual to collective issues. The economy is impressive. The main clause of the passage quoted above is in the optative, its syntax interrupted by a long parenthesis which delays the gesture voiced in the wish ('to wrap him in music'); the parenthesis, by creating an obstacle semantically and grammatically, enables the verse to enact the frustration and tenuousness of the wish involved. Further, the expression 'to wrap him in music' works with superb economy of means to associate an 'ordinary' gesture of a purely physical kind of comfort (a blanket) and the consolation of art (music/poetry).

This 'consolation' is offered in a sense in the next part of the collection, a poem inspired precisely by listening to a piece of music, so that the sombre mourning of 'Laments for a dead Companion' is counterbalanced by what is possibly the most luminous section of

Pensées. The two pieces together represent the extremes of what Jaccottet calls 'le clair et l'obscur' ('light and darkness' in all their senses). They are rarely held in equipoise and their various gradations colour the other sections of the collection. Where music had failed or had offered at most a frail consolation in the Jourdan threnody, in 'To Henry Purcell' it is offered in a sequence of poems which must count among the most affirmative of Jaccottet's whole corpus. The affirmative syntax (attenuated by only one disquieting interrogative in the penultimate poem which harks back to the Jourdan poem – 'And will he hear it as he twists and turns / under the torturer's / always too leisurely hands?') is reinforced by the brevity and concision of the poems. Unlike the landscapes in the rest of the collection there is an absence of mist and obstacle: the music, its composer and performer are celebrated (constellated) in the setting of a clear and unimpeded skyscape with constellations (Cygnus and Lyra) that suggest a recurrent figure of desire in Jaccottet's writing: the clear passage into a world after death conferred by the power – Orphic, if we follow the connotations of the Lyre and the general context – of music and poetry. The pact between the two arts is signalled by the implied mutual recognition of poet and composer in the last poem. The constellated night sky offers the model of a redemption and it counterbalances the more threatening image of the sky offered in the first poem of the 'Things seen' sequence right at the beginning of the volume: 'L'énorme enclume qui étincelle d'étoiles' / 'the giant anvil throwing off sparks and stars', yet another of the meticulous cross-references punctuating this poetry.

The most ecstatic part of *Pensées sous les nuages* is followed by 'Le poète tardif...' / 'The poet, late in the day...', the coda to the collection. It summarises the stances already implicit in the voice that articulates the collection as a whole and is a typical gesture of self-evaluation in an ironical, deprecatory third person. Jaccottet likes pronominal shifts: they deflate the possible dangers of lyrical effusion in the first person by introducing ironic distance, and suggest that the self is just one more piece of the natural world under review. This final poem puts into proportion both the self and the activity of the poet, its style more appealing perhaps than earlier pronouncements in the same vein, such as the frequently invoked 'L'effacement soit ma façon de resplendir' / 'Let self-effacement be my means of resplendence', where ambition arguably carries the day over modesty. 'Le poète tardif...' resonates particularly with the eponymous poem 'Pensées sous les nuages' / 'Under clouded skies' where the self is also ironically distanced in an internal dialogue which voices both the ambitiousness of poetry, and the way in which encroaching age and failing ressources endanger that ambition, the journey that is unlikely to be made. If the dominant images of *Pensées sous les nuages* are those of mist and cloud as frustrating obfuscation, fragile possibilities of clarity nevertheless subsist and the writing of poetry persists 'in spite of...' Significantly, the bird has always been one of Jaccottet's recurring figures. Fragile but rapid in its ubiquitous displacements, it measures 'distances' with acuity of eyesight and it sings. Its element is air and it becomes an emblem of the poet dedicated to light:

> L'attachement à soi augmente l'opacité de la vie. Un moment de vrai oubli, et tous les écrans les uns derrière les autres deviennent transparents, de sorte qu'on voit la clarté jusqu'au fond, aussi loin que la vue porte; et du même coup plus rien ne pèse. Ainsi l'âme est vraiment changée en oiseau.

> Self-attachment increases the opacity of things. A moment of real detachment from self and all barriers start falling away into transparency, one behind the other, so that at one and the same time the very heart of light becomes visible and everything stops being weighed down. The spirit really becomes a bird.

> (*La Semaison:* May 1954)

This bird becomes less assured with time. The final image of *Pensées sous les nuages*, the scared bird flying towards the light, encapsulates the tonality and the matter of the whole volume, attesting to the fragile persistence of poetry and leaving a natural sign as signature:

> Il parle encore, néanmoins,
> et sa rumeur avance comme le ruisseau en janvier
> avec ce froissement de feuilles chaque fois
> qu'un oiseau effrayé fuit en criant vers l'éclaircie.

> He continues speaking nevertheless
> and his murmurs come on like a stream in January
> with that troubling of the leaves every time a frightened bird
> takes flight with a cry towards an opening.

Bibliography: Works mentioned and further reading

PHILIPPE JACCOTTET: **Principal Works**

L'Effraie et autres poèmes (Paris: Gallimard, 1953)
La Promenade sous les arbres (Lausanne: Mermod, 1957)
L'Ignorant: poèmes 1952-56 (Paris: Gallimard, 1957)
Éléments d'un songe (Paris: Gallimard, 1961)
L'Obscurité (Paris: Gallimard, 1961)
La Semaison: carnets 1954-62 (Lausanne: Payot, 1963)
Paysages de Grignan (Lausanne: La Bibliothèque des Arts, 1964)
Airs: poèmes 1961-64 (Paris: Gallimard, 1967)
L'Entretien des muses: chroniques de poésie (Paris: Gallimard, 1968)
Gustave Roud (Paris: Seghers, 1968)
Leçons (Lausanne: Payot, 1969)
Paysages avec figures absentes (Paris: Gallimard, 1970)
Rilke par lui-même (Paris: Seuil, 1971)
Poésie: 1946-67 (Paris: Gallimard, Collection *Poésie*, 1971)
La Semaison: carnets 1954-67 (Paris: Gallimard, 1971)
Chants d'en bas (Lausanne: Payot, 1974)
À travers un verger (Montpellier: Fata Morgana, 1975)
À la lumière d'hiver (Paris: Gallimard, 1977)
Journées: carnets 1968-75 (Lausanne: Payot, 1977)
Les Cormorans (Marseille: Idumée, 1980)
Beauregard (Paris: Maeght, 1981)
Pensées sous les nuages (Paris: Gallimard, 1983)
Des histoires de passage: prose 1948-78 (Lausanne: Éditions du Verseau, 1983)
La Semaison: carnets 1954-79 (Paris: Gallimard, 1984)
À travers un verger, suivi de Les Cormorans et de Beauregard (Paris: Gallimard, 1987)
Une Transaction secrète (Paris: Gallimard, 1987)
Autres journées (Montpellier: Fata Morgana, 1987)
Cahier de verdure (Paris: Gallimard, 1990)
Libretto (Geneva: La Dogana, 1990)
Cristal et fumée (Montpellier: Fata Morgana, 1993)
Après beaucoup d'années (Paris: Gallimard, 1994)
Écrits pour papier journal: Chroniques 1951-1970 (Paris: Gallimard, 1994).

PHILIPPE JACCOTTET: Texts in English Translation

Breathings: Translations of Jaccottet Poems, by Cid Corman (New York: Mushinsha-Grossman, 1974)

Seedtime, Extracts of the notebooks 1954-1967, translated by André Lefevere & Michael Hamburger (New York: New Directions, 1977)

Through an orchard, translated by Mark Treharne (Isle of Skye: Aquila, 1978)

Selected Poems, translated by Derek Mahon (Harmondsworth: Penguin Books, 1988)

Cherry Tree, translated by Mark Treharne (Birmingham: Delos Press, 1991)

Further substantial translations of Jaccottet's work can be found in the following reviews: *Modern Poetry in Translation* 16 (1973); *Prospice* 3 (1975); *Scripsi* 3 (1985) and *Scripsi* 4 (1987).

Selected Further Reading on Jaccottet

IN ENGLISH

Andrea Cady: *Measuring the Visible: the Verse and Prose of Philippe Jaccottet* (Amsterdam: Rodopi, 1992)

Richard Stamelman: *Lost Beyond Telling* (Ithaca: Cornell University Press, 1990)

Mark Treharne: 'Reinscription in Jaccottet's *Carnets*: reading *La Semaison*', *French Studies*, 46 (1992), 174-87.

IN FRENCH

Jean-Pierre Richard: *Onze études sur la poésie moderne* (Paris: Éditions du Seuil, 1964)

Jacques Borel: *Poésie et nostalgie* (Paris: Berger-Levrault, 1979)

Jean-Luc Seylaz: *Philippe Jaccottet: une poésie et ses enjeux* (Lausanne: Éditions de l'Aire, 1982)

Marie-Claire Dumas (editor): *La Poésie de Philippe Jaccottet* (Paris: Champion, 1986)

Jean-Pierre Vidal: *Philippe Jaccottet* (Lausanne: Payot, 1989)

Alentour de Philippe Jaccottet, special issue of the review *Sud* no.80/81 (Marseille: 1989)

Other References

John Berger: *The White Bird* (London: The Hogarth Press, 1988)

John Berger: *About Looking* (London, Writers and Readers Publishing Cooperative, 1980)

Friedrich Hölderlin: Poems and Fragments, translated by Michael Hamburger (Cambridge: Cambridge University Press, 1980; London: Anvil Press, 1994)

Pierre-Albert Jourdan: *Les Sandales de paille* (Paris: Mercure de France, 1987)

Pierre-Albert Jourdan: *Le Bonjour et l'adieu* (Paris: Mercure de France, 1991)

Louis Martz: *The Poetry of Meditation* (New Haven and London: Yale University Press, 1962)

Maurice Merleau-Ponty: *Le Visible et l'invisible* (Paris: Gallimard, 1964)

Maurice Merleau-Ponty: *L'Oeil et l'esprit* (Paris: Gallimard, 1964)

Eugenio Montale: *The Coastguard's House*, English version by Jeremy Reed (Newcastle upon Tyne: Bloodaxe Books, 1990)

Octavio Paz: *Le Singe grammairien*, translated by Claude Esteban (Geneva: Skira, 1972)

Francis Ponge: *La Rage de l'expression* (Paris: Gallimard, Collection Poésie, 1989)

Jean-Pierre Richard: *Pages paysages: microlectures II* (Paris: Éditions du Seuil, 1984)

Rainer Maria Rilke: *The Selected Poetry*, edited and translated by Stephen Mitchell (London: Pan Books, 1987)

Giuseppe Ungaretti: *Selected Poems*, edited and translated by Patrick Creagh (Harmondsworth: Penguin Books, 1969)

These translations are dedicated to the memory of Andrea Cady and to Mel.

PENSÉES SOUS LES NUAGES
UNDER CLOUDED SKIES

TRANSLATED BY
DAVID CONSTANTINE & MARK TREHARNE

ON VOIT
THINGS SEEN

On voit les écoliers courir à grands cris
dans l'herbe épaisse du préau.

Les hauts arbres tranquilles
et la lumière de dix heures en septembre
comme une fraîche cascade
les abritent encore de l'énorme enclume
qui étincelle d'étoiles par-delà.

L'âme, si frileuse, si farouche,
devra-t-elle vraiment marcher sans fin sur ce glacier,
seule, pieds nus, ne sachant plus même épeler
sa prière d'enfance,
sans fin punie de sa froideur par ce froid?

Tant d'années,
et vraiment si maigre savoir,
cœur si défaillant?

Pas la plus fruste obole dont payer
le passeur, s'il approche?

– J'ai fait provision d'herbe et d'eau rapide,
je me suis gardé leger
pour que la barque enfonce moins.

We see the schoolchildren who run and shout
in the grassy playing-place.

By the tall calm trees
and the September mid-morning light
as by a cool cascade
they are still shielded from the giant anvil
throwing off sparks and stars in a near distance.

Shy soul, little shivering thing,
must she really walk this glacier eternally,
alone, barefoot, no longer even able
to recite the prayers she knew as a child,
punished eternally for her coldness by this cold?

After so many years
really such meagre knowledge,
faintheart?

Not even the roughest obolus to pay
the ferryman, if he comes?

— I have made a store of grass and hurrying water,
I have kept myself light
so the boat will ride higher.

Elle s'approche du miroir rond
comme une bouche d'enfant
qui ne sait pas mentir,
vêtue d'une robe de chambre bleue
qui s'use elle aussi.

Cheveux bientôt couleur de cendre
sous le très lent feu du temps.

Le soleil du petit matin
fortifie encore son ombre.

Derrière la fenêtre dont on a blanchi le cadre
(contre les mouches, contre les fantômes),
une tête chenue de vieil homme se penche
sur une lettre, ou les nouvelles du pays.
Le lierre sombre croît contre le mur.

Gardez-le, lierre et chaux, du vent de l'aube,
des nuits trop longues et de l'autre, éternelle.

Quelqu'un tisse de l'eau (avec des motifs d'arbres
en filigrane). Mais j'ai beau regarder,
je ne vois pas la tisserande,
ni ses mains même, qu'on voudrait toucher.

Quand toute la chambre, le métier, la toile
se sont évaporés,
on devrait discerner des pas dans la terre humide...

She comes to the mirror.
The mirror is round like a child's mouth
that cannot tell a lie.
She is wearing a blue dressing-gown
it too getting worn.

Hair soon the colour of ash
in the very slow fire of time.

The early morning sun
strengthens her shadow still.

Behind the window whose wood has been whitened
(against the flies, against the ghosts)
an old man is bowing his white head
over a letter or the local news.
Dark ivy grows against the wall.

Save him, ivy and whitewash, from the dawn wind,
from nights that last too long and from eternal night.

Someone is weaving water (motifs of trees
as a watermark). But however I look
I never see the weaver
nor even her hands that we should like to touch.

When the workplace, the loom, the cloth itself
have all evaporated
we ought to discover footprints in the damp earth...

On est encore pour un temps dans le cocon de la lumière.

Quand il se défera (lentement ou d'un seul coup),
aura-t-on pu au moins former les ailes
du paon de nuit, couvertes d'yeux,
pour se risquer dans ce noir et dans ce froid?

On voit ces choses en passant
(même si la main tremble un peu,
si le cœur boite),
et d'autres sous le même ciel:
les courges rutilantes au jardin,
qui sont comme les œufs du soleil,
les fleurs couleur de vieillesse, violette.

Cette lumière de fin d'été,
si elle n'était que l'ombre d'une autre,
éblouissante,
j'en serais presque moins surpris.

For a while we are still inside the cocoon of the light.

When it comes undone (slowly or suddenly)
shall we at least have been able to grow the wings
of a night-flying emperor, covered with eyes,
to take our chance in that darkness and in that cold?

We see these things in passing
(though the hand is a little shaky
and the heart limps)
and others under the same sky:
gourds shining in the garden
like the eggs of the sun,
flowers the colour of old age, a purple.

This light at the end of summer
if it were only the shadow of another,
blinding,
I should almost be less surprised.

PENSÉES SOUS LES NUAGES

UNDER CLOUDED SKIES

– Je ne crois pas décidément que nous ferons ce voyage
à travers tous ces ciels qui seraient de plus en plus clairs,
emportés au défi de toutes les lois de l'ombre.
Je nous vois mal en aigles invisibles, à jamais
tournoyant autour de cimes invisibles elles aussi
par excès de lumière...
                              (À ramasser les tessons du temps,
on ne fait pas l'éternité. Le dos se voûte seulement
comme aux glaneuses. On ne voit plus
que les labours massifs et les traces de la charrue
à travers notre tombe patiente.)

– Il est vrai qu'on aura peu vu le soleil tous ces jours,
espérer sous tant de nuages est moins facile,
le socle des montagnes fume de trop de brouillard...
(Il faut pourtant que nous n'ayons guère de force
pour lâcher prise faute d'un peu de soleil
et ne pouvoir porter sur les épaules, quelques heures,
un fagot de nuages...
Il faut que nous soyons restés bien naïfs
pour nous croire sauvés par le bleu du ciel
ou châtiés par l'orage et par la nuit.)

– Mais où donc pensiez-vous aller encore, avec ces pieds usés?
Rien que tourner le coin de la maison, ou franchir,
de nouveau, quelle frontière?

(L'enfant rêve d'aller de l'autre côté des montagnes,
le voyageur le fait parfois, et son haleine là-haut
devient visible, comme on dit que l'âme des morts...
On se demande quelle image il voit passer

– I am not convinced we shall ever make that journey
across the many skies becoming clearer and clearer,
carried away in defiance of all the laws of shadow.
I cannot see us as invisible eagles
for ever circling the peaks invisible themselves
in the excess of light...
                              (Picking up the broken bits of time
will not construct eternity. We learn to stoop, that is all,
like the gleaners. Now we see
only the massive ploughlands and the marks of the plough
across our patient tomb.)

– True, we have seen little of the sun lately
and it is less easy to hope under such an amount of cloud,
the mountain platform billows with too much fog...
(But how nearly destitute of strength we must be
if we let go for want of a bit of sun
and are incapable of shouldering
a fardel of clouds for an hour or so...
And we must be very naive still
to think ourselves saved by the blue of the sky
or punished by storms and night.)

– Where else did you think you were going on your worn feet?
Only rounding the house or crossing
a border – which? – again?

(The child dreams of going to the other side of the mountain.
A traveller may, and his breath up there
shows, as they say that the souls of the dead...
We ask ourselves what image he sees passing

dans le miroir des neiges, luire quelle flamme,
et s'il trouve une porte entrouverte derrière.
On imagine que, dans ces lointains, cela se peut:
une bougie brûlant dans un miroir, une main
de femme proche, une embrasure...)

Mais vous ici, tels que je vous retrouve,
vous n'aurez plus la force de boire dans ces flûtes de cristal,
vous serez sourds aux cloches de ces hautes tours,
aveugles à ces phares qui tournent selon le soleil,
piètres navigateurs pour une aussi étroite passe...

On vous voit mieux dans les crevasses des labours,
suant une sueur de mort, plutôt sombrés
qu'emportés vers ces derniers cygnes fiers...

– Je ne crois pas décidément que nous ferons encore ce voyage,
ni que nous échapperons au merlin sombre
une fois que les ailes du regard ne battront plus.

Des passants. On ne nous reverra pas sur ces routes,
pas plus que nous n'avons revu nos morts
ou seulement leur ombre...
                          Leur corps est cendre,
cendre leur ombre et leur souvenir; la cendre même,
un vent sans nom et sans visage la disperse
et ce vent même, quoi l'efface?
                          Néanmoins,
en passant, nous aurons encore entendu
ces cris d'oiseaux sous les nuages
dans le silence d'un midi d'octobre vide,
ces cris épars, à la fois près et comme très loin

in the mirror of the snows, what flame he sees glimmering,
and whether he finds a door half open at the back.
We imagine that in those distances it might be so:
a candle burning in a mirror, the hand
of a woman close, an opening...)

But you, such as I find you here,
you will no longer have the strength to drink from those crystal flutes,
you will be deaf to the bells of those high towers,
blind to those beacons that turn as the sun turns,
unfit for the navigation of such narrow straits...

Easier to imagine you labouring in crevasses of clay
sweating the death-sweats, foundering,
not lifted up towards those proud and final swans...

– I am not convinced we shall make that journey now
nor escape the shadow of the axe
once the wings of sight have ceased to beat.

Passers-by. We shall not be seen on these roads again
any more than we have ever seen our dead
or even their shades...
                    Their bodies are ash,
ash their shades and their memory and the ashes themselves
a nameless faceless wind disperses them
and the wind itself, what effaces it?
                    Nonetheless
in passing we shall have heard again and still
these bird-cries under the clouds
in the silence of an empty October noon,
these scattered cries, near and yet seeming very far away

(ils sont rares, parce que le froid
s'avance telle une ombre derrière la charrue des pluies),
ils mesurent l'espace...
                    Et moi qui passe au-dessous d'eux,
il me semble qu'ils ont parlé, non pas questionné, appelé,
mais répondu. Sous les nuages bas d'octobre.
Et déjà c'est un autre jour, je suis ailleurs,
déjà ils disent autre chose ou ils se taisent,
je passe, je m'étonne, et je ne peux en dire plus.

(they are rare because the cold
advances like a shadow behind the ploughing rain),
they measure space...
                                And passing underneath them
it seems to me they have spoken, not asked anything or called
but answered. Under the low clouds of October.
Already it is another day and I am elsewhere,
already they are saying something else or have fallen silent.
I pass, I am amazed, I can say nothing more about it.

LE MOT JOIE
THE WORD JOY

Je me souviens qu'un été récent, alors que je marchais une fois de plus dans la campagne, le mot joie, comme traverse parfois le ciel un oiseau que l'on n'attendait pas et que l'on n'identifie pas aussitôt, m'est passé par l'esprit et m'a donné, lui aussi, de l'étonnement. Je crois que d'abord, une rime est venue lui faire écho, le mot soie; non pas tout à fait arbitrairement, parce que le ciel d'été à ce moment-là, brillant, léger et précieux comme il l'était, faisait penser à d'immenses bannières de soie qui auraient flotté au-dessus des arbres et des collines avec des reflets d'argent, tandis que les crapauds toujours invisibles faisaient s'élever du fossé profond, envahi de roseaux, des voix elles-mêmes, malgré leur force, comme argentées, lunaires. Ce fut un moment heureux; mais la rime avec joie n'était pas légitime pour autant.

Le mot lui-même, ce mot qui m'avait surpris, dont il me semblait que je ne comprenais plus bien le sens, était rond dans la bouche, comme un fruit; si je me mettais à rêver à son propos, je devais glisser de l'argent (la couleur du paysage où je marchais quand j'y avais pensé tout à coup) à l'or, et de l'heure du soir à celle de midi. Je revoyais des paysages de moissons en plein soleil; ce n'était pas assez; il ne fallait pas avoir peur de laisser agir le levain de la métamorphose. Chaque épi devenait un instrument de cuivre, le champ un orchestre de paille et de poussière dorée; il en jaillissait un éclat sonore que j'aurais voulu dire d'abord un incendie, mais non: ce ne pouvait être furieux, dévorant, ni même sauvage. (Il ne me venait pas non plus à l'esprit d'images de plaisir, de volupté.) J'essayais d'entendre mieux encore ce mot (dont on aurait presque dit qu'il me venait d'une langue étrangère, ou morte): la rondeur du fruit, l'or des blés, la jubilation d'un orchestre de cuivres, il y avait du vrai dans tout cela; mais il manquait l'essentiel: la plénitude, et pas seulement la plénitude (qui a quelque chose d'immobile, de clos, d'éternel), mais le souvenir ou le rêve d'un espace qui, bien que plein, bien que complet, ne cesserait, tranquillement, souverainement, de s'élargir, de s'ouvrir, à l'image d'un temple dont les colonnes (ne portant plus que l'air ainsi qu'on le voit aux ruines) s'écarteraient à l'infini les unes des autres sans rompre leurs invisibles liens; ou du char d'Élie dont les roues grandiraient à la mesure des galaxies sans que leur essieu casse.

Ce mot presque oublié avait dû me revenir de telles hauteurs comme un écho extrêmement faible d'un immense orage heureux. Alors, à la naissance hivernale d'une autre année, entre janvier et mars, à partir de lui, je me suis mis, non pas à réfléchir, mais à écouter et recueillir des signes, à dériver au fil des images; comprenant, ou m'assurant paresseusement, que je ne pouvais faire mieux, quitte à n'en retenir après coup que

I remember that in a recent summer, whilst I was out walking in the country yet again, there came to mind, rather as a bird might pass across the sky without our expecting or being at once able to identify it, the word 'joy' and, as the bird might, it too astonished me. I think that then, as though belonging to it like an echo or a rhyme, another word joined it, the word 'silk'; and not quite without reason, for the summer sky at that moment, shining, light and precious, put me in mind of immense banners of silk floating over the trees and the hills with silvery reflections whilst from a deep ditch choked with reeds bullfrogs I still could not see were lifting up voices which were, though loud, nevertheless as if silvery or lunar. It was a happy moment; but all the same the association of the two words could not be justified.

The word itself, the word which had surprised me and whose sense, as it seemed to me, I no longer fully grasped, was round in the mouth, like a fruit; if I began to dwell on it I should have to slip from silver (the colour of the landscape in which I was walking when I suddenly thought of it) into gold, and from the evening hour into the hour of noon. I recalled harvest landscapes in full sunlight; that was not enough; I had to risk letting the leaven of metamorphosis work. Each ear of corn became an instrument of brass, the field an orchestra of straw and gilded dust; fountains of bright sound rose up from it, like a fire, as I was first inclined to say, but no: it was wrong to think of fury or of anything devouring or even wild. (Nor did any images of pleasure of an erotic kind occur to me.) I tried to listen even more closely to the word (which almost seemed to have come to me from a foreign language or a dead language): the roundness of fruit, the gold of corn, the jubilation of an orchestra of brass, in all that there was some truth; but the essential thing was missing: plenitude, and not only plenitude (which has something immobile, closed and eternal about it), but the memory or the dream of a space which, although full, although complete, would still in a calm and sovereign fashion continue to be enlarged and to open, like a temple whose columns (no longer bearing anything but the air, as is the case with ruins) went infinitely far apart from one another without ever breaking their invisible connections; or like the wheels of the chariot of Elijah growing to be as big as galaxies and yet their axle never snapping.

That almost forgotten word must have come back to me from heights such as those, like the extremely faint echo of an immense storm of happiness. Then at the winter birth of another year, between January and March, having the word as my starting point, I began I cannot say to reflect but to listen and to gather signs and to follow wherever the images led me; knowing, or out of laziness telling myself, that I could do no des fragments, même imparfaits et peu cohérents, tels, à quelques ratures près, que cette fin d'hiver me les avait apportés – loin du grand soleil entrevu.

better, resigned to retaining only fragments after all, imperfect ones at that and scarcely coherent, just as, give or take a few crossings-out, that end of winter had brought me them – a long way from the great sun I had glimpsed.

Je suis comme quelqu'un qui creuse dans la brume
à la recherche de ce qui échappe à la brume
pour avoir entendu un peu plus loin des pas
et des paroles entre des passants échangées...

(Celui qui n'y voit plus très bien, qu'il se fie à l'enfant
pareille à l'églantier...
Il fait un pas dans le soleil de fin d'hiver
puis reprend souffle, risque encore un pas...

Il n'a jamais été vraiment attelé à nos jours
ni libre comme qui s'ébroue dans les prairies de l'air,
il est plutôt de la nature de la brume,
en quête du peu de chaleur qui la dissipe.)

I am like a man digging in the mist
for something evading even the mist
after hearing steps a little way ahead of me
and words exchanged by passers-by...

(If you can no longer see very well in there
trust to the child
a girl like the wild roses...
He takes a step in the end-of-the-winter sun
and gets his breath, and risks another step...

He has never been really harnessed to our times
nor free and capable of frolicking on the prairies of the air,
his nature is rather like the mist's
in search of the little warmth that will disperse it.)

Toute joie est très loin. Trop loin probablement déjà,
comme il se dit qu'il l'a toujours été, même enfant,
s'il se rappelle mieux le parfum d'une pivoine humide
effleurée alors du genou
que le visage de sa mère jeune
dans le jardin où le cormier tachait l'allée de rouge.

Lui qui ne va plus même jusqu'au fond de son jardin.

Tel le coureur à bout de forces
passe à celui qui le relaie un bâton de bois blanc,
mais sa main tient-elle rien encore à passer derrière lui,
nulle branche pour refleurir ou pour brûler?

All joys are very distant. Doubtless already too distant,
he thinks, having been himself
even as a child too distant
since he remembers the scent of a damp peony
brushed by his knee in those days
better than he does the face of his young mother
in the garden where the service tree stained the path red.

And he never even goes to the bottom of his garden now.

He is like the runner at the end of his strength
passing on a baton of white wood to be carried beyond him,
but does his hand still hold nothing to leave behind him,
no branch that might flower again or burn?

L'aurais-je donc inventé, le pinceau du couchant
sur la toile rugueuse de la terre,
l'huile dorée du soir sur les prairies et sur les bois?

C'était pourtant comme la lampe sur la table avec le pain.

Rappelle-toi, au moment de perdre pied,
puise dans cette brume avec tes mains affaiblies,
recueille ce peu de paille pour litière à la souffrance,
là, au creux de ta main tachée:

cela pourrait briller dans la main
comme l'eau du temps.

Am I to believe I invented it then,
the brush of the sunset over the rough canvas of the earth,
the golden oil of evening over the fields and the woods?

Yet it was like the lamp on the table with the bread.

Remember as you lose your footing,
dip into this mist with your weakened hands,
gather these bits of straw for bedding under your griefs,
there, in the hollow of your mottled hand:

it might shine in the hand
like the water of time.

Jour à peine plus jaune sur la pierre et plus long,
ne vas-tu pas pouvoir me réparer?
Soleil enfin moins timoré, soleil croissant,
ressoude-moi ce cœur.

Lumière qui te voûtes pour soulever l'ombre
et secouer le froid de tes épaules,
je n'ai jamais cherché qu'à te comprendre et t'obéir.

Ce mois de février est celui où tu te redresses
très lentement comme un lutteur jeté à terre
et qui va l'emporter –
soulève-moi sur tes épaules,
lave-moi de nouveau les yeux, que je m'éveille,
arrache-moi de terre, que je n'en mâche pas
avant le temps comme le lâche que je suis.

Je ne peux plus parler qu'à travers ces fragments pareils
à des pierres qu'il faut soulever avec leur part d'ombre
et contre quoi l'on se heurte,
plus épars qu'elles.

O daylight a little yellower and longer on the stone
will you not be able to mend me?
Sunlight at last less timid, o increasing sun
solder my heart again.

Light stooping to lift the shadows
and to shake the cold from your shoulders
I never sought anything but to understand you and obey you.

This February month is when you get to your feet
very slowly like a wrestler thrown
and now about to win –
lift me on to your shoulders,
wash out my eyes again so that I wake,
wrest me from the dirt to stop me eating it
before I have to, coward that I am.

My only way of speaking is through fragments which are like
stones that must be lifted with their share of shadow
and against which we stumble
being more scattered than they are.

Mais chaque jour, peut-être, on peut reprendre
le filet déchiré, maille après maille,
et ce serait, dans l'espace plus haut,
comme recoudre, astre à astre, la nuit...

(Prière des agonisants: bourdonnement
d'abeilles noires, comme pour aller recueillir
au plus profond de fleurs absentes
de quoi faire le miel dont nous n'avons jamais goûté.

Ainsi écoute-t-on la voix de ces moines
qui vivaient sur le toit du monde
au fond de temples pareils à des forts
dressés sur le passage des vents inconnus
dont leurs conques ramassent la violence.

Leur gong tonne
ou c'est un glacier qui se fend.

Eux-mêmes chantent de la voix la plus puissante
et la plus basse jamais entendue,
on croirait des bœufs ruminant leurs psaumes,
attelés à plusieurs pour labourer sans relâche
le champ coriace de l'éternité.

Erraient-ils, à tirer ainsi leur charrue à soc de glacier
de l'aube au soir?

Leurs voix à la mesure des montagnes
les tenaient-elles en respect?

On les écoute maintenant de loin,
nous les bègues à la voix brisée,
dispersée comme paille au moindre souffle.)

74

But perhaps every day we can gather up again
the torn net, stitch by stitch,
and it would be, in the higher spaces,
like sewing the night together star by star...

(Death-bed prayers: a droning
of black bees, as if to go and gather
in the deepest depths of absent flowers
something to make the honey we never tasted.

In that way we listen to the voices of the monks
who lived on the roof of the world
in the depths of temples which resemble fortresses
raised up on the route of unimaginable winds
whose violence they gathered in a conch.

Their gong thunders
or is it a glacier splitting?

Theirs is the mightiest singing voice
and the deepest ever heard.
They ruminate their psalms like oxen yoked
several together to plough without respite
the ungiving fields of eternity.

Were they wrong to drag from dawn to dusk
a plough that had a glacier for its share?

And surely their voices, as large as the mountains,
commanded the mountains' respect?

We listen to them now at a distance.
We are the stammerers with broken voices,
voices the least breeze scatters like straw.)

Dans la montagne, dans l'après-midi sans vent
et dans le lait de la lumière
luisant aux branches encore nues des noyers,
dans le long silence:
le murmure de l'eau
qui accompagne un instant le chemin,
l'eau décelable à ces fétus brillants,
à ces éclats de verre dans la poussière,
sa claire et faible voix
de mésange apeurée.

Ce matin, il y avait un miroir rond dans la brume,
un disque argenté près de virer à l'or,
il eût suffi d'yeux plus ardents pour y voir
le visage de celle qui en efface avec un tendre soin
les marques de la nuit...

Et dans le jour encore gris
courent ici et là comme la crête d'un feu pâle
les branchages neufs des tilleuls...

In the mountains in the windless afternoon
and in the milk of the light
shining on the still bare branches of the walnut-trees
in the long silence:
the murmur of water
accompanying the path for a little while
water discernible in brilliant wisps
in glassy sparkles in the dust
its clear and feeble voice
like a frightened tom tit's.

This morning there was a round mirror in the mist,
a silvery disc on the verge of becoming golden.
Intenser eyes would have seen in it
the face of the woman who gently, carefully,
wipes away the marks of the night...

And in the still grey daylight
here and there like the crest of a pale flame
the running of the new shoots on the lime trees...

Comme on voit maintenant dans les jardins de février
brûler ces petits feux de feuilles
(et l'on dirait que c'est moins pour nettoyer
le clos que pour aider la lumière à s'élargir),
est-il bien vrai que nous ne pouvons plus
en faire autant, avec notre cœur invisible?

Regarde-la courir sur ses jambes toutes nouvelles
à la rencontre de l'amour
comme un ruisseau de verre tintant sur les roches,
pleine de hâte et de rire!

Est-ce le fouet des hirondelles sur les prés humides
qui la presse?

Maintenant nous montons dans ces chemins de montagne,
parmi des prés pareils à des litières
d'où le bétail des nuages viendrait de se relever
sous le bâton du vent.
On dirait que de grandes formes marchent dans le ciel.

La lumière se fortifie, l'espace croît,
les montagnes ressemblent de moins en moins à des murs,
elles rayonnent, elles croissent elles aussi,
les grands portiers circulent au-dessus de nous –
et le mot que la buse trace lentement, très haut,
si l'air l'efface, n'est-ce pas celui que nous pensions
ne plus pouvoir entendre?

Qu'avons-nous franchi là?
Une vision, pareille à un labour bleu?

Garderons-nous l'empreinte à l'épaule, plus d'un instant,
de cette main?

See now in the February gardens
little fires of leaves burning
(and less, as it seems, to tidy up
our plot than to help the light increase):
Is it really beyond us now to do likewise
with our invisible hearts?

See her running after love
light on her feet again
like tinkling glass, like a stream over the stones,
full of haste and laughter!

Maybe the whiplash of swallows over the wet fields
is hurrying her.

Now we are climbing these mountain paths
through meadows where clouds
were sleeping like cattle till the herdsman came,
the wind with his stick.
Large shapes seem to be marching in the sky.

Light strengthens, space is growing,
the mountains are less and less like walls,
they shine, they are growing too,
the guardians of the entrances are doing the rounds above us –
and the word the buzzard writes unhurriedly and very high
if the air erases it, still
was it not the word we thought we could never hear again?

What have we entered here?
A vision, like blue ploughlands?

Shall we feel for more than a moment
where that hand touched our shoulders?

Il se dessine une veine rose dans l'air
et peu à peu plusieurs, comme sous la peau
d'une main jeune qui salue ou dit adieu.
Il s'insinue une douceur dans la lumière
comme pour aider à traverser la nuit.

Autant de plumes, tourterelle, pour tes ailes,
autant de rumeurs tendres à tes lèvres, inconnue.

Il y a la peine, qui ravine,
il y a le froid qui gagne,
quelquefois c'est comme si l'on n'avait plus de peau,
seulement la pierre des os:
une cage de pierre avec au centre un foyer froid,
une espèce de geôle où l'on ne sait
s'il y a quelqu'un encore à délivrer,
et la clef heurtant les barreaux
fait un bruit dur et mat.

La peine a pris racine avec des cordes jaunes
comme l'ortie
et le visage s'est assombri.
Il est des plantes si tenaces
que le feu seul peut en avoir raison.

A vein of rose is traced in the air
and little by little several, as under the skin
of a young hand greeting or saying goodbye.
A gentleness enters the light
as if it would help us through the night-time.

So many feathers for the wings of the dove,
so many soft whispers
for the lips of the woman still without a name.

There is a sorrow digging furrows
and the cold is getting the upper hand,
sometimes it seems the skin has gone
and there is only the stone of the bones:
a cage of stones and a cold hearth at the centre
a sort of prison from which
there may or may not be a prisoner still to deliver,
and the key hitting the bars
makes a hard dull sound.

Sorrow has rooted, like nettles,
with yellow cords
and the face has gone into shadow.
There are plants so tenacious
only fire can defeat them.

On dirait qu'il se cache, avec effroi, dans la lumière de l'aurore
comme au fond d'une roseraie;
il y respire un tel parfum
qu'il lui semble, à sa suite, échapper aux barreaux de brume.

Ah! comme il la regarde, cette aurore,
ce peu de braise dans le fer des montagnes,
celui qui s'en éloigne un peu plus chaque matin!
Comme il se souvient! Comme il se souvient mal:
quand le visage, quand le corps aussi devenait rose
au premier vague cri d'oiseau aventuré!

Les nuages se bâtissent en lignes de pierres
l'une sur l'autre,
légère voûte ou arche grise.

Nous pouvons porter peu de chose,
à peine une couronne de papier doré;
à la première épine
nous crions à l'aide et nous tremblons.

Qu'on me le montre, celui qui aurait conquis la certitude
et qui rayonnerait à partir de là dans la paix
comme une montagne qui s'éteint la dernière
et ne frémit jamais sous la pesée de la nuit.

In the light of the dawn he is like a man hiding
frightened, in the depths of a rose garden;
he breathes such scents in there
he seems to be escaping with them through the bars of the mist.

How he stares at the dawn,
the bit of heat and light in the iron of the mountains
and every morning he leaves it further behind.
How he remembers things! Remembers things badly:
when the face, when the body too had the flush of roses
when the first bird bravely uttered its vague cry.

The clouds are building, one on the other,
like courses of stone,
light vaults or grey arches.

We can bear very little
scarcely even a paper crown;
on thorny ground
at once we cry for help and tremble.

I should like to see the man who had got possession of certainty
and shone forth from it even as far as peace
like a mountain the last to lose its light
and never quailing under the weight of the night.

Cette montagne a son double dans mon cœur.

Je m'adosse à son ombre,
je recueille dans mes mains son silence
afin qu'il gagne en moi et hors de moi,
qu'il s'étende, qu'il apaise et purifie.
Me voici vêtu d'elle comme d'un manteau.

Mais plus puissante, dirait-on, que les montagnes
et toute lame blanche sortie de leur forge,
la frêle clef du sourire.

On ouvre de nouveau les grands livres:
ceux qui parlent de châteaux à enlever, de fleuves
à franchir, d'oiseaux qui serviraient de guides...

Leurs paroles,
on les dirait prises dans les plis d'étendards bleus
qu'un vent venu on ne sait d'où exalte
au point qu'on n'y peut lire aucune phrase jusqu'au bout.

Ou l'on croirait qu'elles marchent entre des cimes,
elles-mêmes immenses, à peine ouïes, inaccessibles,
à moins qu'à la chaleur du cœur
elles ne retombent en neige sur nos pieds nus.

This mountain has its double in my heart.

I lean against its shadow,
I collect its silence in my hands
to have that silence grow in me and outside me
and spread and soothe and purify.
So I am dressed in the mountain as in a cloak.

But mightier perhaps than the mountains
and any white blade from their forge:
the frail key of a smile.

We open the great books again
that speak of castles to capture, rivers
to cross, birds who would serve as guides...

Their words seem caught in the folds of blue banners
lifted by a wind come from who knows where
so we can never read a sentence to the end.

Or they seem to be walking among mountain tops,
being themselves immense, scarcely heard, inaccessible,
unless in the warmth from our hearts
they fall again as snow on our bare feet.

Cette lumière qui bâtit des temples,
ces colonnes bleues sur leurs socles de pierre
au pied desquels nous avons marché pleins de joie

(sur la table rugueuse ayant déposé quelques simples
en figure d'étoiles poussiéreuses,
ayant trempé nos mains dans l'auge des bêtes
comme en un sarcophage d'eaux étincelantes),

cette lumière souveraine sur les rocs,
portant au centre du fronton le disque en flammes
qui aveugle nos yeux,

si elle est sans pouvoir, comme il semble, sur les larmes,
comment l'aimer encore?

La lyre de cuivre des frênes
a longtemps brillé dans la neige.

Puis, quand on redescend
à la rencontre des nuages,
on entend bientôt la rivière
sous sa fourrure de brouillard.

Tais-toi: ce que tu allais dire
en couvrirait le bruit.
Écoute seulement: l'huis s'est ouvert.

This light, the builder of temples,
these blue columns on their pedestals of stone
below which we walked full of joy

(having laid a few herbs on the rough table
in the shapes of dusty stars,
having dipped our hands in the trough where the beasts drink
as in a sarcophagus of sparkling waters),

this sovereign light on the stones,
bearing full in its pediment the disc of flames
which blinds our eyes,

can we still love a light
that seems to have no power over tears?

The copper lyre of the ashtrees
has shone for a long time in the snow.

Then, going down to meet the clouds again,
soon you hear the river
under its wrap of mist.

Say nothing: what you were going to say
would drown the sound.
Only listen: the doors have opened.

À UNE JEUNE MÈRE
TO A YOUNG MOTHER

Toi que j'entends pleurer, fille de Sion,
au bord de ce berceau où se mirait ton sourire
et qu'a tari maintenant l'été sévère,
endure! que ta plainte ne se change pas
en cris à déchirer le ciel.

Quelqu'un pourrait venir qui lierait la gerbe de tes larmes.

(Sa meule tourne depuis toujours entre les astres.)

Qui sait, alors, si tu n'auras pas repris goût
à ce pain qu'il t'apporte au lever du jour?

Daughter of Zion whom I hear weeping
over the cradle where your smile was mirrored as in a pool
now the harsh summer has dried it up
have courage still and do not let your lament
become a cry that would rip the heavens apart.

Someone might come who will bind up the sheaf of your tears.

(His mills grind as they always have among the stars.)

Who knows: by then
perhaps you will have an appetite again
for the bread he brings you at daybreak.

PLAINTES SUR UN COMPAGNON MORT

LAMENTS FOR A DEAD COMPANION

En voici un de plus qui entre dans le défilé
à peu de pas, peut-être, devant nous.

D'effroi ravalé, sa peau tressaille près de l'œil.

Les paroles si pures dont il se vêtait
tombent en loques.

Ah! tendez-lui encore un verre plein de l'air du soir,
gardez-le encore un moment de cette suie qui encrasse
les rochers rapprochés.

Nous ne l'aurons pas suivi bien loin.

Je ne peux presque plus chanter, dit le chanteur,
on a tranché les racines de ma langue.
Je ne vois pas plus loin que ces ombres qui avancent,
on a tranché les racines de mes yeux.

Feuilles et nuages
avec votre face de nuit et l'autre de jour,
prairies profondes, lointains de plus en plus larges,
on aura beau vous regarder, vous questionner,
si vous n'êtes que feuilles et nuages, herbes et collines,
vous ne nous êtes pas d'un grand secours.
Un simple coup de vent un peu frais vous éteint,
comme sur nous ces peines froides
font passer l'ombre de la faux.

Était-ce bien la peine de paraître la lumière
si l'on ne peut servir de baume
dès que l'outil de la souffrance creuse un peu profond?

Here's yet another who has entered that narrow way
perhaps only a few steps ahead of us.

The skin around his eyes is twitching with swallowed fear.

The words he wore, of such purity,
have gone to rags.

Oh, let him be given once more a glass full of the evening air,
a little longer keep him from touching the soot
caked on the closing walls.

We shan't have been far behind.

I can scarcely sing anymore, says the singer,
they have severed the roots of my tongue.
I can see no further than these shadows which are getting nearer,
they have severed the roots of my eyes.

Leaves and clouds
with your night face and the other, your day face,
deep fields, wider and wider distances,
it will be of no use to look at you and question you,
if all that you are is leaves and clouds and grass and hills.
By any brisker than usual gust of wind you are effaced,
as over us these cold troubles
cause the shadow of the scythe to pass.

Was it worth our efforts at clarity
if we can be of no solace
as soon as the instrument of suffering digs at all deep?

On voudrait, pour ce pas qu'il doit franchir
– si l'on peut parler de franchir
là où la passerelle semble interrompue
et l'autre rive prise dans la brume
ou elle-même brume, ou pire: abîme –
dans ce vent barbelé,
l'envelopper, meurtri comme il l'est, de musique...

Et ce n'est pas qu'aucune musique protège
de pareilles morsures;
plutôt qu'elle soulève, qu'elle incline différemment
et qu'elle semble dire, quelquefois:
«Où je vous porte, si vous m'écoutez,
le pire froid, la pire ombre ne sont bientôt plus
que vieilles hardes par vous oubliées
comme peau de serpent dans les pierres après la mue,
l'inouï dont je suis l'écho répercuté
par les sombres parois grandit et gagne,
comme vous avez vu gagner le jour
sur les replis les plus profonds de la vallée...»

Se pourrait-il qu'ainsi enveloppé
il cesse de trembler
et ne soit plus rompu et terrassé qu'en apparence?

Vous, lentes voix qui vous nouez et dénouez
dans le ciel intérieur,
si vous ne mentez pas, enlevez-le dans vos mailles
plus limpides que celles de la lumière sur les eaux.

One would like, for the crossing he has to make
– if we can speak of a crossing
when the bridge seems broken off
and the other bank in a mist
or itself a mist, or worse, an abyss –
in this barbed-wire wind
to wrap him in music, hurt as he is...

Not that there is a music which can shield us
against such bites;
but that music lifts, it inclines us differently
and seems to say, sometimes:
'Where I may carry you, if you will listen,
the worst cold, the worst darkness will soon be only
rags you discard
like the skin of a snake sloughed off among the stones,
and the unheard things, whose echo I relay,
grow between the sombre walls and advance
as you have seen the daylight advance
over a valley's deepest folds...'

Might it not be that wrapped like this
he would stop trembling
and be only in appearance broken and beaten down?

Slow voices ravelling and unravelling
in the heaven inside
if you are telling the truth abduct him in your nets
that are more limpid than those of light over water.

(Je parle d'encore plus bas, là où la peur me gagne
au point que, pour un peu, je me tairais.)

Comme il aura duré, l'interrogatoire!
Je l'ai vu entre deux séances, dans un répit:
ils ne l'avaient pas ménagé.

Que T'avait-il donc fait, Commissaire aux astres?
Il Te cherchait. Tu lui as rompu les artères.

Et la lumière ne s'est même pas voilée
au-dessus du coffre sombré.

(I am speaking of even lower down, down there where fear
so seizes me I shall soon be mute.)

How it must have lasted, his questioning!
I saw him between two sessions, in a respite:
they had not been gentle with him.

But what had he done to You, Commandant of the Stars?
He was seeking You. You broke his veins.

Nor was there even a veil
over the light when the box went down.

À HENRY PURCELL

TO HENRY PURCELL

Écoute: comment se peut-il
que notre voix troublée se mêle ainsi
aux étoiles?

Il lui a fait gravir le ciel
sur des degrés de verre
par la grâce juvénile de son art.

Il nous a fait entendre le passage des brebis
qui se pressent dans la poussière de l'été céleste
et dont nous n'avons jamais bu le lait.

Il les a rassemblées dans la bergerie nocturne
où de la paille brille entre les pierres.
La barrière sonore est refermée:
fraîcheur de ces paisibles herbes à jamais.

Ne croyez pas qu'il touche un instrument
de cyprès et d'ivoire comme il semble:
ce qu'il tient dans les mains
est cette Lyre
à laquelle Véga sert de clef bleue.

À sa clarté,
nous ne faisons plus d'ombre.

Listen: how can it be
that our troubled voices are mingling like this
with the stars?

He has made them scale the sky
on rungs of glass
by the youthful grace of his art.

He has allowed us to hear the passing of ewes
their press through the dust of a celestial summer
bearers of milk that we have never drunk.

He has gathered them in the night-time fold,
there is a shine of straw among the stones.
The sonorous gate has closed:
freshness of peaceful pasture now for ever.

Do not suppose he is fingering an instrument
of cypress and ivory, as it seems:
what he has in his hands is the Lyre
whose clef is blue Vega.

We are no longer
a shadow on its brightness.

Songe à ce que serait pour ton ouïe,
toi qui es à l'écoute de la nuit,
une très lente neige
de cristal.

On imagine une comète
qui reviendrait après des siècles
du royaume des morts
et, cette nuit, traverserait le nôtre
en y semant les mêmes graines...

Nul doute, cette fois les voyageurs
ont passé la dernière porte:

ils voient le Cygne scintiller
au-dessous d'eux.

Listening in to the night
imagine you heard
a snowing of crystal
a very slow fall.

Imagine a comet
come back from the kingdom of the dead
after centuries away
and tonight it crosses our kingdom
sowing the very same seeds...

It is certain that this time the travellers
have passed through the final door:

they see the Swan
a sign
shining beneath them.

Pendant que je t'écoute,
le reflet d'une bougie
tremble dans le miroir
comme une flamme tressée
à de l'eau.

Cette voix aussi, n'est-elle pas l'écho
d'une autre, plus réelle?
Va-t-il l'entendre, celui qui se débat
entre les mains toujours trop lentes
du bourreau?
L'entendrai-je, moi?

Si jamais ils parlent au-dessus de nous
entre les arbres constellés de leur avril.

Tu es assis
devant le métier haut dressé de cette harpe.

Même invisible, je t'ai reconnu,
tisserand des ruisseaux surnaturels.

As I listen to you
the reflection of a candle
is trembling in the mirror
like a flame plaited
with water.

Is not this voice also the echo
of another, more real?
And will he hear it as he twists and turns
under the torturer's
always too leisurely hands?
And shall I?

If ever they converse above us
among their April's constellated trees.

You are seated
before the high loom of your harp.

I recognised you though you were invisible
weaver of the supernatural streams.

LE POÈTE TARDIF...
THE POET, LATE IN THE DAY...

Le poète tardif écrit:

«Mon esprit s'effiloche peu à peu.

Même la passerose et la mésange me semblent lointaines,
et le lointain de moins en moins sûr.

J'en arriverais presque à demander
qu'on me décharge de ce sac de lumière:
drôle de gloire!»

Qui de vous, beautés, répondra?

N'en sera-t-il pas une d'entre vous
pour, même sans rien dire, se tourner vers lui?

Comme il s'égaille, le troupeau des sources
qu'on avait cru conduire un jour dans ces prairies...

Voila que désormais
toute musique de jadis lui monte aux yeux
en fortes larmes:

«Les giroflées, les pivoines reviennent
l'herbe et le merle recommencent,
mais l'attente, où est-elle? Où sont les attendues?
N'aura-t-on plus jamais soif?
Ne sera-t-il plus de cascade
pour qu'on en serre de ses mains la taille fraîche?

Toute musique désormais
vous bâte d'un faix de larmes.»

Il parle encore, néanmoins,
et sa rumeur avance comme le ruisseau en janvier
avec ce froissement de feuilles chaque fois
qu'un oiseau effrayé fuit en criant vers l'éclaircie.

He writes:

'My spirit is fraying.

Even the hollyhock and the blue tit seem to me distant
and the distance less and less sure.

I am near to asking
to be unburdened of this charge of light:
a queer sort of glory!'

Among the beauties will any give an answer?

Will even one among them,
wordless if need be, turn his way?

How it scatters, the flock at the water sources
we thought to conduct into our fields one day...

Now any music from an earlier time
comes to his eyes
as copious tears:

'The stocks and the peonies return,
the grasses and the blackbird begin again
but where is the waiting and the expectation? Where
are the women waited for?
Shall we never again be thirsty?
Will there never again be a waterfall,
to hold its cool waist between our hands?

Now every music
saddles you with a burden of tears.'

He continues speaking nevertheless
and his murmurs come on like a stream in January
with that troubling of the leaves every time a frightened bird
takes flight with a cry towards an opening.

Note

On voit, Septembre – octobre 1976.
Paru, à l'exception d'un poème, dans *Argile*, XI, automne 1976.

Pensées sous les nuages, Octobre 1976.
Paru dans *Argile*, XVIII, hiver 1978-1979.

Le mot joie, Janvier 1981 – janvier 1982.

À une jeune mère, Août – septembre 1981.

Plaintes sur un compagnon mort, Juillet – décembre 1981.
À la mémoire de Pierre-Albert Jourdan.

À Henry Purcell, Septembre 1981.
Après un concert de James Bowman à Saint-Julien-le-Pauvre. Paru dans la NRF, nº 351, avril 1982.

Le poète tardif…, Décembre 1981 – janvier 1982.

Note

Things seen, September – October 1976.
Appeared, minus one poem, in *Argile*, XI, Autumn 1976.

Under clouded skies, October 1976.
Appeared in *Argile*, XVIII, Winter 1978-1979.

The Word Joy, January 1981 – January 1982.

To a young mother, August – September 1981.

Lament for a dead Companion, July – December 1981.
To the memory of Pierre-Albert Jourdan.

To Henry Purcell, September 1981.
Written after a James Bowman concert at Saint-Julien-le-Pauvre. Appeared in the *Nouvelle revue française*, No. 351, April 1982.

The poet, late in the day..., December 1981 – January 1982.

BEAUREGARD

TRANSLATED BY
MARK TREHARNE

BEAUREGARD

BEAUREGARD

Encore une chose vue par hasard, à la fin d'un voyage d'hiver – et au surplus une chose notée plus d'une fois déjà, interrogée déjà: à ce moment d'avant la nuit, de transition, où il y a du vert sombre (toujours chargé de sens à mes yeux), du rose et du jaune comme d'un feu – et dans le village (dont j'ai retrouvé plus tard le nom sur la carte: Beauregard), les premières lampes derrière les carreaux. Un relais entre le jour et la nuit. Mais à cela s'ajoutaient ici deux éléments particuliers: d'abord, une grande carrière creusée dans le flanc de la colline; et c'était la carrière qui s'allumait, entaille monumentale; ensuite, la situation même de ce village à l'entrée d'un défilé, dans une région où les collines, les montagnes s'élèvent de plus en plus haut les unes derrière les autres comme une succession de décors, la première chaîne étant souvent interrompue par ces gorges étroites où l'on rêve immanquablement de s'engager. Encore une histoire de passage...

Village perdu, presque un hameau, inconnu (mais il s'agissait bien de Beauregard, dans la Drôme), insignifiant, du moins pour qui n'y vit pas: je ne m'y suis jamais arrêté. Quelques maisons seulement, mais habitées, puisqu'on a vu s'y allumer les premières lampes; et on ne sait rien de ce qu'elles éclairent, mais on ne le devine que trop aisément: les visages fatigués ou mornes, les mains usées, les assiettes sur la table miroitante (on a vendu ou brûlé celle en bois), la vie tempérée d'aujourd'hui, un peu vide, à moins qu'elle ne dissimule une violence souterraine, qui explosera plutôt en désespoir qu'en éclats de joie. Toutefois, on allume les lampes et cela aide, tandis que le vert des prairies et des forêts devient comme de l'encre ou presque, s'imprègne de nuit; et qu'à l'inverse, une dernière fois avant la nuit, flamboie l'entaille de la carrière, à croire qu'on aurait allumé là-bas un grand brasier rose qui semble sourdre de la terre elle-même – et c'est aussi comme un verre de lumière à boire, un verre de soleil couchant. (Ainsi deux mondes se lient-ils l'un à l'autre, se relaient-ils mutuellement.) Au delà, les montagnes ont bâti un mur, et il y a une porte dans ce mur. Le village garde la porte (l'a gardée, il y a longtemps). Plus personne ne passe là; du moins, plus d'envahisseurs, de brigands, plus d'ours ni de loups par grand froid; même plus de fantômes? Mais c'est resté une porte qu'un enfant rêve encore d'ouvrir, de franchir, justement peut-être quand la nuit comme aujourd'hui tombe, et quand s'allume la carrière, le feu autour duquel il n'y a plus personne, et qui ne réchauffe un instant, de loin, que le voyageur.

118

Yet again something seen by chance, at the end of a winter jour-
ney – what is more, something already noted more than once, already
questioned: the moment before nightfall, a transition, coloured with
dark green (always charged with meaning for my eyes), pink and
the yellow of a fire – and in the village (Beauregard: I found the
name later on the map) the first lamplight in windows. A point of
transition between day and night. There were two further distinctive
features: the one, a large quarry dug out of the hillside, a massive
gash which was beginning to light up; the other, the very position
of the village at the entrance of a narrow gorge in a region where the
hills, then the mountains, rise higher and higher behind each other
like a succession of stage decors, the first range often broken by
those narrow passes which never fail to lure the imagination. Once
more, the old story of passing beyond...

A remote village, little more than a hamlet, unknown (but there
it was, Beauregard in the Drôme), insignificant, at least to those
who do not live in it: I have never stopped there before. Merely a
few houses, yet lived in, since the light of those first lamps was
there; you know nothing of what they illuminate but can imagine
only too easily: the tired or sad faces, the worn hands, the plates on
the formica table (the wooden one burnt, or sold), the tempered life
of today, rather empty, except for those hidden sources of violence
which tend to explode into despair rather than into outbursts of
joy. Yet the lamps are lit and that helps: meanwhile the green of
the fields and forests turns almost to ink, soaks up the dark night;
and by contrast, for the last time before nightfall, the gash in the
quarry flares up with light, as if someone had lit a huge pink fur-
nace which seems to well up from the earth itself – a proffered
glass of light, a drink of setting sun. (Two worlds joining, taking
over from each other.) Further back the mountains have built a wall
and there is a gate in the wall. The village guards the gate (has
done so for a long time). No one passes through it any more: at
least no invader, no bandit, no bear or wolf in times of severe cold;
no ghost even? Yet the gate is still there, like the gate a child dreams
of opening and passing through, the more so perhaps when dark-
ness falls as it does today and the quarry lights up, a fire around
which no one any longer stands, warming for a second, and from
afar, only the traveller.

Là s'allumait un feu, au milieu des choses encrées par la nuit imminente, à côté de ce seuil — comme pour le signaler au regard. C'était la lampe du gardien. Le rocher s'enflammait, s'était enflammé doucement (on voit aussi cela sur des visages — également dans la proximité de la nuit), quelqu'un faisait un feu qui ne semblait pas du tout dévorant, qui n'avait rien d'un fauve aux aguets, si beau cela soit-il aussi, c'était un feu posé contre le rocher comme une première floraison de pêchers en mars, cela n'allait durer qu' un instant, le temps pour le voyageur (en rêve) de s'approcher du seuil du défilé, de s'y engager; et alors, très vite, l'ombre et le froid l'envelopperaient et il serait amené à presser le pas, peut-être aurait-il peur de se perdre, à moins que le bruit d'une rivière en contre-bas ne lui servît d'autre guide, plus invisible, plus fidèle. De l'autre côté du défilé, cependant, il n'y aurait rien, le jour revenu, qui ne fût aussi en deçà — à peine plus de silence et de solitude: quelques fermes plus éparses et un peu plus haut sur des coteaux plus dénudés, à l'ombre d'un seul grand tilleul, dans de larges prairies; et de nouveau, mais plus proche, plus escarpée, la pente de la montagne surplombée de rochers, le ciel lui-même comme en surplomb; et, le cas échéant, quelqu'un dans un petit jardin potager ou sous un hangar qui vous saluerait distraitement ou, s'il vous parlait un instant, ne dirait aucune parole autre que celles entendues la veille; de sorte qu'il semblerait peut-être n'avoir pas valu la peine de faire tant de pas ou d'avoir nourri un quelconque espoir...

Mais pourquoi, comment cet espoir était-il né? On peut se demander, non seulement pourquoi on avait cédé à son invite une fois de plus, après autant de déceptions que d'entreprises ou de pas, mais comment l'invite même avait été possible, et ce que sa possibilité veut dire...S'apercevrait-on alors qu'y obéir n'était pas nécessaire, qu'entrer était superflu, que le passage s'était opéré en vous au moment où sa seule pensée s'était fait jour dans votre cœur, que le passage réel était en deça du seuil, de ce côté-ci, c'était la lampe allumée contre la paroi de rocher et la porte dans la forêt; que ce feu allumé par personne, apparu au regard de quelqu'un d'étranger à ce lieu et emporté par sa voiture tout à fait ailleurs et dans une tout autre histoire, était lui-même le passage, pas simplement un signe, un appel, une proposition — et même au contraire: une réponse, un don au-delà desquels il ne fallait rien chercher, parce que toute la substance du monde est en eux, le temps qu'on l'aperçoive — après quoi toute la cendre nocturne peut tomber sur vous, il faudra bien qu'elle se soit d'abord envolée de ce brasier silencieux.

A fire was alight there, amid a world inked over by oncoming night, beside a threshold – as if to draw one's eye to the spot. The watchman's lamp. The rock was bursting into flame, had gently burst into flame (you see that in human faces too – likewise at the approach of night); someone was building a fire which had nothing devouring about it, nothing of the wild beast on the prowl (whatever the beauty of that too); it was a fire set against the rock like the first blossoming of peach trees in March and it would only last for a second, the time it took for the traveller (in dream) to approach the threshold of the pass and to enter; and then, rapidly, shadow and cold would envelop him and he would be forced to walk on more hastily, perhaps frightened of getting lost, unless the sound of a river below were to offer another sort of guidance, more invisible, more trustworthy. On the other side of the pass nonetheless, with the return of daylight, there would be nothing that was not already on this side of it – scarcely more silence or more solitude: a few farms, more scattered and slightly higher up on barer slopes, shaded by one tall lime tree, set in broad fields; and once again, but closer, steeper, there would be the slope of the mountain overhung with rocks and the sky itself almost like an overhang; and maybe someone in a small kitchen garden or a barn who would make a vague gesture of greeting or, were he to exchange a few words, would say nothing that you had not heard the evening before; so that it would perhaps not seem to have been worth the effort to have walked so far or to have nurtured some sort of hope...

Yet why, and how, was such a hope born? You can ask not only why the invitation had been accepted once again, after as many disappointments as journeys undertaken, but also what had made the invitation itself possible and what its possibility could mean...Would it then become clear that to follow it was unnecessary, that to enter was superfluous, that the idea of passage had occurred at the moment when the mere thought of it had dawned in your heart, that the real idea of passing beyond existed this side of the threshold, here where you stand – it was there in the lamplight against the rockface and the gateway into the forest; that the fire lit by no one and becoming visible to someone who was a stranger to this place, carried off in a car to somewhere quite different and into an utterly different life, was itself the passage, not merely a sign, a call, a beckoning – perhaps just the opposite – a reply, a gift beyond which nothing more was needed, because the whole substance of the world is contained in such things at the very moment they are perceived – and then, even if all the ashes of night were to fall on you, they would have been blown in the first place from this silent fire.

Beauregard: c'était donc le nom de ce village, et il me revient aujourd'hui en l'écrivant que j'ai toujours aimé ce mot, que depuis l'enfance il a été pour moi comme une invite, un signe; parce qu'il y avait un tel lieu-dit aux abords de ma petite ville natale, ce devait être une ferme ou un domaine sur la pente qui descend vers la Broye (je pourrais m'en informer, mais peu importe), je me souviens simplement de ce nom comme s'il avait eu une résonance plus riche que d'autres, et pas même, je crois, à cause de son sens implicite, simplement «comme ça», pour rien; comme si, quand on disait «Beauregard» autour de moi dans la vaste maison toujours froide en hiver dès que l'on s'éloignait des hauts poêles de faïence dont certains prétendaient même tiédir deux pièces à la fois, quand on disait ce mot, on faisait tinter une cloche justement pour accéder à quelque lieu inconnu que je n'aurais sûrement pas trouvé si j'étais allé vraiment me promener près de cette ferme, de ce domaine. Oui, ce mot tintait comme un instrument de métal frappé par un marteau – et dont le retentissement, maintenant que j'y songe après tant d'années, n'était pas sans analogie avec celui (qu'on imagine) d'un gong dans la cour d'un temple d'Asie, ou celui des sonnailles d'un troupeau qu'on entend avant de le voir, tels des œufs de fourmis sur un lointain versant de haute montagne – et le son clair se répand, vient à vous à travers la distance elle-même absolument claire, c'est l'air lui-même qui tinte et vibre, l'air tout à fait invisible des hauteurs qui semble s'ouvrir à son passage – tandis que les montagnes s'élèvent immobiles, à distance les unes des autres, comme des beffrois.

Beauregard... Je me souviens aussi maintenant, en poursuivant ma rêverie, d'un poème de Montale, *Tempi di Bellosguardo*, dont longtemps je me suis contenté d'aimer le titre à cause de ce même mot, alors que le poème lui-même est très beau (*O come nella corusca | distesa che s'inarca verso i colli, | il brusio della sera s'assottiglia...*); et il s'agit là d'un quartier de Florence, avec tout ce qui s'ébranle en moi à la moindre allusion à l'Italie (pays auquel je n'aurai jamais su rendre l'hommage que je lui dois depuis plus de trente ans que je m'y suis rendu pour la première, merveilleuse, lointaine fois); mais là, il s'agit plus précisément, plus étymologiquement d'une «vue» que l'on a d'un lieu magiquement nommé ainsi sur un paysage, comme d'une galerie, d'un balcon où l'on se tient à la fin du jour, et vos

Beauregard: this then was the name of the village, and today as I write the word down I remember that I have always been fond of it, that since my childhood it has been like an invitation, a sign to me; because there was just such a named locality near the small town where I was born, it must have been a farm or an estate on the slope which goes down towards La Broye (I could find out, but it does not matter), I simply remember the word as if it were more richly resonant than others and not even, I think, because of its implicit meaning, simply 'because...', for no reason at all; as if, whenever I heard someone say 'Beauregard' in that vast house which was always cold in winter the moment you moved away from the glazed earthenware stoves, some of which were even supposed to heat two rooms at once – whenever I heard the word, it was exactly as if a bell were rung to gain access to some unknown place which I would certainly not have discovered by actually walking near the farm or the estate in question. Yes – the word resonated like a metal instrument struck by a hammer – and its resonance, now I come to think about it after so many years, was not unlike the sound (as I imagine it) of a gong in the court of an Asian temple, or the tinkling bells of cattle, heard before they are seen, ants' eggs on a far-off slope deep in the mountains – and the clear sound spreads, comes towards you through the distance, itself utterly clear, the air itself ringing and vibrating, the utterly invisible air of the heights which seems to open to the passing sound – and the mountains rise motionless, distant one from the other, like belfries.

Beauregard... I am reminded too, as I let my thoughts wander, of a poem by Montale, *Tempi di Bellosguardo*, which I loved for a long time simply for its title, because it contained the same word; and yet the whole poem is very fine (*O come nella corusca | distesa che s'inarca verso i colli, | il brusio della sera s'assottiglia...*). It is about a district of Florence with everything that stirs inside me at the least mention of Italy (a country I will never be able to pay the homage I have owed it since I went there over thirty years ago for the first time – marvellous, remote); but the poem, in a more precise, more etymological sense, concerns the 'view' of a landscape from a place thus magically named, seen as if from a gallery or a balcony where you are standing at the end of a day and your eye drinks in yeux boivent silencieusement tout cela, le cœur s'étonne, la pensée s'éveille: on aura vu cela, mais qu'aura-t-on vu? Et pourquoi? Si bien qu'on se retourne vers la personne peut-être assise en retrait dans l'ombre et qui bientôt, disant qu'il fait un peu froid, va rentrer dans la chambre, à moins qu'elle ne soit encore penchée tout près de vous sur la balustrade de vieux fer: on voit alors ses yeux saturés de la lumière du monde sur lesquels rapidement les paupières se baissent pour ne plus laisser filtrer qu'un désir de tendresse ou de long sommeil. Se fermeraient-elles tout à fait que ce serait une nuit difficile à franchir. Ainsi continue-t-on d'errer, bien qu'on n'en ait plus guère le temps ni peut-être le droit, de source en source, comme une ombre falote en quête de vie, de plus en plus vacillante, déracinée, boiteuse, à l'image des papillons de nuit; jusqu'à ce que se dresse sur son chemin le mur qu'aucune magie de parole n'aide plus à contourner ou à ouvrir.

the whole scene in silence, in astonished emotion, and your thoughts stir: this has been seen, but what has been seen? and why? so that you finally turn round to the person who may be sitting back there in the shade and will soon return to the bedroom saying that she finds it has turned rather cold, or who might be leaning right beside you on the old iron balustrade: and then you notice her eyes drenched in the light of the world, over which her eyelids are quickly lowered to filter nothing more than the desire for love or long sleep. Were those eyelids to close for ever, the night to be lived through would be hard. So one continues to wander, with scarcely the time or perhaps the right to do so any more, from source to source, like a pale shadow seeking after life, more and more faltering, uprooted and clumsy, like a moth; until there looms upon the path the barrier which no magic of words can any longer help to circumvent, or to open up.

TROIS FANTAISIES
THREE FANTASY PIECES

Mars

Voici sans doute les dernières neiges sur les versants nord et ouest des montagnes, sous le ciel qui se réchauffe presque trop vite; il me semble cette année que je les regretterai, et je voudrais les retenir. Elles vont fondre, imprégner d'eau froide les prés pauvres de ces pentes sans arbres; devenir ruissellement sonore ici et là dans les champs, les herbes encore jaunes, la paille. Chose elle aussi qui émerveille, mais j'aurais voulu plus longtemps garder l'autre, l'aérienne lessive passée au bleu, les tendres miroirs sans brillant, les fuyantes hermines. J'aurais voulu m'en éclairer encore, y abreuver mes yeux.

Lettres de l'étranger...

Je laisse, à ma manière paresseuse, circuler ces images, espérant parmi elles trouver la bonne, la plus juste. Qui n'est pas encore trouvée, et ne le sera d'ailleurs jamais. Parce que rien ne peut être identifié, confondu à rien, parce qu'on ne peut rien atteindre ni posséder vraiment. Parce que nous n'avons qu'une langue d'hommes.

Bourgeons hâtifs, pressés, promptes feuilles, verdures imminentes, ne chassez pas trop vite ces troupes attardées d'oiseaux blancs. Ces ruches de feuilles – et là-haut, loin, ces ruches de cristal.

(Ici, de nouveau, surgissent les couleurs, sur fond de terre, à l'abri des cyprès, dans leur enclos sombre; le troupeau des couleurs, des fleurs – et il y a aussi les feux des saules, une charrette, un homme accroupi, travaillant on ne sait à quoi, un arrosoir. Le rose insaisissable, jailli, suspendu: vol arrêté. Dans l'abri, derrière les barrières vertes, ces braises qui ne brûlent pas si on les prend dans sa main, mais s'y éteignent vite. L'aube des arbres, du bois. Comme il est étonnant que cela doive se changer bientôt en fruit rond et lourd, tels des œufs d'oiseaux...Arbre un instant couvert d'ailes, qui vont tomber, jaunir, s'éparpiller, se remélanger à la terre encore humide.)

March

These are no doubt the last snows on the north and west slopes of the mountains, beneath a sky which is warming up almost too soon; I feel I shall miss them this year and I want to keep them there. They are going to melt and the cold water will soak into the sparse meadows on these treeless slopes, turn to sonorous streaming here and there in the fields, in the still yellow grasses, in dead grass. This in itself is a marvel but I would have preferred to hold on to the other one for longer: the whites of the air passed through the washing-blue, the soft, lustreless mirrors, the fleeing ermine. I would have liked to live longer in their light, to drench my eyes in it.

Letters from abroad...

In my lazy way, I let these images circulate in the hope that I shall discover the right one, the most appropriate one. I have not discovered it yet, nor will I ever. Because nothing can be identified with anything else, not utterly, because nothing can be reached or possessed completely. Because our only language is human language.

May the hurried early buds, the leaves which come so swiftly, the imminent green, not chase away too soon these lingering flocks of white birds. Hives of leaves – and high up over there, hives of crystal.

(Down here, colours are welling up once more against a background of earth, shaded by cypresses in their dark enclosure; the flock of colours, of flowers – and also the fire of the willows, a cart, a figure crouched over some job of work, a watering-can. The elusive rose colour, bursting out, suspended: arrested flight. Sheltered behind green barriers, the embers that do not burn the hand that holds them but die out swiftly. The dawn of the trees, of the wood. How astonishing it is that all this will soon turn to rounded heavy fruit, like birds' eggs...a tree covered for one moment in wings and the next those wings are going to fall, turn yellow, scatter and mingle once more with the still damp soil.)

129

Là-haut, ces abeilles froides – chassées par celles du soleil. Je voudrais marcher là-haut maintenant, atteindre le bord de ces miroirs, de ces lacs qui se résorbent lentement, y plonger le visage – au-dessus des arbres et des fleurs.

Les neiges vont fondre, elles commencent à fondre – elles sont effacées par la tiédeur de l'air piqué de cris d'oiseaux comme une étoffe, bientôt elles ruisselleront, sonores, dans la paille des champs, elles descendront, viendront à nous, rapides, froides, limpides – bondissantes, elles vont se dénouer comme des nuages – ah! qu'on regarde encore cela, qu'on le recueille et le respire. Ce sont les cimes qui se dénouent et ruissellent et courent vers nous (mais c'est bien autre chose, je dois seulement laisser le flot passer, les eaux courir, descendre, m'alimenter).

Sources suspendues, cimes devenues sources – allumées autour de nous très haut. Une lumière que l'altitude et le froid cristallisent et soudain, ou peu à peu, la saison venue, elle quitte ces hauteurs, se dénoue et vient à nous, rapide et gaie, une bousculade amortie par les herbes.

Neige qui se décoiffe, dépeignée en ruisseaux, neige que les nœuds du froid tenaient serrée – et, retire-t-on ces peignes, ces épingles, elle croule, elle ruisselle en mèches vives, parfumées – toutes les eaux fraîchement crépitantes du printemps dans les prés.

Continuerais-je ainsi, je crois que je ne tarderais pas à murmurer un nom, plusieurs noms peut-être, de ceux que je n'ai pas dits assez haut quand je l'aurais pu, trop avare ou trop soucieux que j'étais de ma vie. L'âge froid commence qui, lui, ne connaîtra pas d'heureuse débâcle, de dégel, du moins sur le versant visible de ce monde-ci; et je le surprends de plus en plus souvent à s'égarer dans des rêveries qui remontent le temps pour en oublier l'irrésistible et indéviable courant, et déboucher en amont sur une source qui prend divers visages, quelquefois très vagues ou tout à fait incon-

Up there, those bees of the cold – chased away by the bees of the sun. I want to be walking up there now, to reach the edge of those mirrors, of the lakes which are gradually being absorbed into the earth, to plunge my face into them – up there above trees and blossoms.

The snows will melt, are beginning to melt – effaced by the warmth of the air stitched with bird cries like a piece of cloth, and soon they will stream down, sonorous, into the dead grass of the fields, they will come down to us, swift, cold and clear – will untangle themselves like clouds, in leaps and bounds – and may we look at all this while it is still there, absorb it, breathe it in. Mountain tops falling loose, streaming down and rushing towards us (but it is not that at all, I must simply let the flow pass by, let the water run down and nourish me).

Hanging springs, summits changed to springs – lit up around us on the far heights. Light turned to crystal by height and cold, then suddenly, or more gradually, with the change of season, it leaves the heights, falls loose and comes towards us, in rapid laughter, a muffled scurry in the grasses.

Snow loosening its hair, combing it out into streams, snow that was braided tight by the winter cold – and once the combs and pins are removed, it falls free, streams into live, scented strands of hair – all the freshly trickling waters of Spring in the fields.

Were I to continue in this manner I think I would soon be murmuring a name, perhaps several names, among the ones I have never uttered loud enough before, when I could have done, too guarded or too anxious as I was about my personal life. Now the cold of old age is beginning to approach and it will find no relief in a drift of melting ice, in friendly thaw, at least not on any visible slope of this world; more and more often I come across it straying into daydream, going back into the past, trying to forget the irresistible and unflinching course of time, and emerging upstream in a source with many nus, mais ce sont toujours des visages – et plus seulement des eaux, fraîches et vives. La figure et l'eau lointaine sont comme tressées ensemble, l'eau n'est plus que du lierre autour de son corps ou une dentelle, et l'âge, caché dans l'embrasure, je le surprends déjà qui épie, se souvient, regrette peut-être ou se reprend à rêver...

Mais je m'approche à nouveau maintenant de cet œuf blanc dans le nid de la brume. La légère troupe féminine s'égaille et je n'entends presque plus le grelot de ses rires. Je me tiens un peu plus tranquille dans cette lumière de mars qu'un rien semble pouvoir briser.

Sources nouées par le froid, par la hauteur, à la limite entre ciel et montagne, je n'ai pas tort de vous confondre avec la lune, ou de vous y rattacher. Vous me lavez les yeux. Je reçois ainsi parfois votre ablution, je ferme les paupières, je les relève: il me semble que mon regard porte un peu plus loin, qu'il me précède et que je dois le suivre.

Je garderai cette obole blanche pour le passeur qu'il n'y a plus.

faces – sometimes very indistinct or completely unknown, but they are always faces – no longer simply fresh, running waters. The face and the distant water are almost braided together, the water is now mere ivy around the figure's body, or lace, and old age is lurking in the space between where I can already catch it spying, remembering, maybe regretting, or beginning to dream again...

But I come back once again now towards the white egg in its nest of mist. The weightless company of feminine presences is scattering and I can now barely hear their jingling laughter. I stand a little more calmly in this March light which the least thing, it seems, could shatter.

Springs braided by winter, by height, at the boundary of sky and mountain, I am not wrong to confuse you with the moon, nor to associate you with her. You cleanse my eyes. In this way I sometimes receive your ablution, I close my eyes, I open them: and it seems that my gaze carries a little further, moves ahead of me, and that I must follow it.

I shall keep this white obol for the boatman who is no longer part of our world.

Avril

Un chercheur d'herbe...touchant la terre encore mouillée allumant de pctits feux de branches, déplaçant des pierres. Sous ces arbres, entre ces buissons et ces haies qui portent déjà presque trop de feuilles, formant des espèces de dômes ou de cages, mais que le plus faible souffle agite et entrouvre. Et lui, cette année plus qu'en aucune autre, comme bousculé par cette hâte, et ce qu'il aurait voulu saisir est déjà passé, changé, disparu.

Il y a là des fleurs couleur orange, une couleur qui n'est ni du feu ni du sang, plutôt parente du soleil, d'un soleil apprivoisé, calmé, une couleur simple, unie, sans profondeur – comme une bonté, un réconfort. Dans l'air ensoleillé mais resté froid.

Lui, il n'a pas plus de réalité que les ombres légères des feuilles, il ignore s'il est même l'ombre de quoi que ce soit; il voudrait être aussi plein, aussi réel que ces fleurs. Par moments, on croirait qu'il leur abandonne sa vie, comme un aveugle se laisse conduire par une enfant.

Des iris aussi se sont ouverts. Il y revient toujours, se fiant à leurs lanternes mauves. S'il y avait une éternité, leur parfum en pourrait être le fil invisible. S'il a eu une vie, c'est leur parfum qui en a tramé l'étoffe, peut-être.

Les lignes du râteau peignent la terre, la rident comme une eau. Il faut les tracer quand celle-ci n'est pas trop sèche, sinon de la poussière s'élève et envahit la maison, se déposant sur les tables, les livres, les flacons. Des moines, en Extrême-Orient, ont créé des jardins de méditation à partir de ces lignes et de quelques pierres. Cela ne me surprend pas, car les dessins du râteau produisent une sorte d'apaisement intérieur, un sentiment de plénitude silencieuse. Pourquoi? Ai-je coiffé la terre comme je coiffe encore quelquefois mon enfant, qui n'est plus une enfant?

Ce travail facile, ces gestes qui s'accommodent de la lenteur et de la distraction, brisent la mince écorce que la chaleur avait rendue imperméable, opaque; on voit de nouveau la matière plus sombre, intime, vivante de la terre. Celle-ci s'est rouverte en même temps qu'elle s'est ordonnée. Ressemblerait-elle à ces persiennes qui laissent passer la lumière en la striant? Je ne sais trop. Sans doute

April

A seeker after grass...touching the still sodden earth, lighting small fires of branches, dislodging stones; beneath these trees, between the bushes and hedges which are already almost too laden with leaves and shaped like domes or cages, yet stirred and half opened by the feeblest breath of wind. And he, more than ever this year, almost jostled by such haste, when what he wanted to grasp has already passed by, changed and gone.

There are orange-coloured flowers now, a colour neither of fire nor of blood, but related more to the sun, a tamed, calmed sun, a simple colour, plain, without depth – like a kindness, a comfort. In air filled with sunlight but still cold.

He is himself no more real than the faint shadows of the leaves, uncertain even whether he is the shadow of anything at all; he would like to be as fully alive, as real as these flowers. At times he seems to entrust his life to them, like a blind man led by a young girl.

Irises have opened. He always returns to them, putting his trust in their mauve lanterns. If there were such a thing as eternity their scent could be its invisible thread. If he has had a life, their scent has woven its fabric...perhaps.

The lines made by the rake comb the soil into ripples like water. They need to be traced when the earth is not too dry or else dust rises and invades the house, falling on tables, books and bottles. In the Far East monks have created gardens for meditation using the lines left by the rake and a few stones. I can understand that, because the raked patterns produce a kind of inner appeasement, a feeling of silent fulfilment. Why? Have I been combing the the earth as I still sometimes comb my child's hair – and she no longer a child?

This simple work, these gestures which require only slowness and distraction, break through the thin bark which the heat had made impermeable and opaque; the darker substance of the earth, more intimate and alive, becomes visible again. It has reopened and ordered itself at the same time. Like blinds letting light through their slats perhaps? I'm not sure. It would be better to think of faut-il plutôt penser à des ondes, à la vibration d'une voix, à l'écriture d'un chant...On aurait fait apparaître un chant à la surface de ce sol qui nous porte et nous recevra; et une fois que c'est achevé, comme devant une surface de neige fraîche, on hésite à y marquer son pas. J'ai fait de ma tombe une chevelure, un lac sombre ou un chant à bouche fermée.

Terre navigable, comme si le vent la ridait.

N'oublie pas que tu as marché dans ce jardin. La maison, dedans, est comme un rocher creux qui en émerge. On ne peut dire ce qu' elle protège, ce qu'elle enferme. À l'intérieur, tout ne saurait être toujours clair et facile. Mais c'est le secret de ceux qui en ont fait leur abri entre deux logements plus opaques. Moi, je puis parler seulement de ce qui tremble et jaillit autour comme l'écume au pied des écueils: iris, lierre et laurier. Arbres et pierres durent plus longtemps que les locataires, les jardiniers. Aussi les aident-ils quelquefois à surmonter leurs craintes, leurs découragements. On soulage certains maux avec des décoctions de plantes sans apparence. J'essaie d'en faire infuser de plus magiques que la sarriette ou même la belladone, puisqu'elles devraient permettre à la plaie la plus profonde de se cicatriser.

Les linaires, dites aussi, je ne sais pourquoi, «ruines de Rome», envahissent les murs comme de légers acrobates à bout de tiges; ou comme de tranquilles essaims d'abeilles un peu pâles, couleur de soir, de souvenirs qui s'effacent; des abeilles qui se seraient endormies en oubliant leur affairement, leur dard et leur miel.

Quand le vent herse l'air, toute la verdure n'est plus que froides étincelles. Les arbres gardent en leur centre comme une réserve de nuit, mais sur leurs bords, en surface, ils multiplient le jour par autant de morceaux de verre, à la fois filtres et miroirs.
Le ciel devient plus bleu, plus dur, plus massif à mesure que l'œil monte et s'éloigne des choses dans leur halo de lumière. Un homme qui a tiré sa chaise au soleil avec la lenteur des malades peu sûrs de guérir parle de son chien, de ses fleurs. Cette voix humaine toute seule dans l'éclat intense de l'après-midi est étrange comme une cloche lointaine.

waves, of the vibrations of a voice, the notation of a song...A song seems to have been made to appear on the surface of the earth which supports us and will receive us; once the work is done, like a stretch of freshly fallen snow, you hesitate to mark it with your footprints.

From my grave I have made combed hair, a dark lake or a song from silent lips.

Navigable earth, as if it were rippled by the wind.

Do not forget that you have walked in this garden. The house inside it seems to emerge out of it like a hollow rock. You cannot say what it protects, what it encloses. Things cannot always be entirely clear and simple within its walls. But that is the secret of the people who have decided to live there, between two darker dwellings. Personally I can only speak of the things that tremble and spring up around the house like surf around a reef: irises, ivy and oleander. Trees and stones live longer than the tenants, the gardeners. But they also, on occasion, help them to overcome their fears and discouragements. Certain sicknesses are relieved by decoctions made from insignificant plants. I try to make infusions from things more magical than savory or even belladonna since they should be able to help the deepest of wounds to heal over.

Toadflax, known also for some reason as 'ruins of Rome', overruns the walls like delicate acrobats at the tips of their stalks; or like tranquil swarms of rather pale bees, the colour of dusk, of fading memory; like bees who have fallen asleep forgetting their bustling activity, their sting and their honey.

When the wind harrows the air every bit of greenery turns to a shower of icy sparks. The trees retain a sort of reserve of darkness at their centre but the outer branches multiply daylight in so many pieces of glass – filters and at the same time, mirrors.

The sky turns bluer, harsher and more massive as the eye looks higher and leaves behind the things that are haloed in light. A man who has drawn his chair into the sun with the slow gestures of someone who is ill and unlikely to recover talks about his dog and his garden. This single human voice amid the intense afternoon brilliance is as strange as the sound of a distant bell.

Prenez cela au moins avant d'être jetés à terre, recueillez ces images, poursuivez ces menus travaux. J'aurais aimé écrire une ode à ce jardin comme certains l'ont fait à l'automne ou à l'âme humaine; et quand on les lit, on éprouve une grande joie. Mais il semble que ce ne soit plus possible, même à de mieux armés que moi. On ouvre la bouche pour célébrer avril, et sur ces mêmes lèvres pèse déjà l'ombre des feuillages d'été. Mais est-ce vraiment la raison? Peut-être l'élan qui porte au chant sait-il déjà qu'il ne durera pas jusqu' au bout de la page, que la dernière, ou même l'avant-dernière ligne ne sera plus que bafouillement?

Aujourd'hui, je dirai seulement de ce jardin que j'y ai vu, d'année en année, la lumière circuler comme un enfant qui jouerait. D'année en année, c'est vrai, je la voyais moins bien, j'avais plus de peine à la suivre, à lui parler. Mais elle jouait toujours sous les feuillages accrus, sans rides, elle, sans cicatrices et sans larmes. Parce qu'elle est entre les choses, elle paraît inaltérable, éternelle même. Et c'est grâce à ces verdures fragiles, à ces jardins changeants, précaires, qu'on la voit. Qu'on y repense un instant entre deux pensées plus sombres ou plus avides. Les plantes murmurent sans cesse de la lumière. Il faudrait trouver ce qui dirait Dieu, ou du moins une joie suprême. L'obstacle, l'écran qui les révélerait.

At least accept all this before you are cast to the ground, pursue these common tasks. I would have liked to write an ode to this garden like those that have been dedicated to autumn or to the human spirit; odes which convey a great joy. But such a thing no longer seems possible, even for writers better equipped than myself. The lips open to celebrate April and on those same lips summer leaves already cast the weight of their shadow. Yet is this the real reason? Perhaps the urge to sing is already the awareness that the song will not last through to the end of the page; the last line, or even the one before, will be no more than gibberish.

For the time being I shall simply say of this garden that from year to year I have seen the light wandering about inside it like a child at play. From year to year, in fact, I have seen it less clearly, found it more difficult to follow and to converse with. By contrast, the light itself continued to play there beneath the accumulating mass of foliage, unwrinkled, unscarred and untearful. By living in between things, it seems to be unchanging, even eternal. Fragile greenery, changing and precarious gardens are things that enable us to see and to think of the light again for a second between two more sombre or more pressing thoughts. Plants never stop murmuring light. That which would speak of God or at least of a supreme joy has still to be discovered. Like finding the obstacle, the screen which would reveal them.

Mai

J'ai dit une fois le pré de mai, une fête gaie et fragile, mais aujourd'hui ce n'est pas le même, ni à la même heure; ce sont plutôt des prés, plus vagues, plus vastes, et qui sont vus non pas en plein soleil, mais le soir; dans un vallon où les terres malgré les drainages sont restées humides, vite détrempées, et où semblent flotter de grands buissons sauvages mais d'une forme régulière, telles des coupoles abritant un chœur de rossignols, entre des murs bas et des chemins eux-mêmes herbeux, sous un ciel gris.

Encore une chose qui me surprend quand je passe, qui me touche de sa flèche tendre et presque silencieuse, qui me sollicite – et je ressens déjà qu'elle sera parmi les plus difficiles à dire, étant des plus discrètes et communes.

De hautes graminées mobiles, légères, d'espèces diverses (qu'il ne servirait sûrement à rien de distinguer, de nommer), et parmi elles des fleurs jaunes, ou roses, indistinctes, nombreuses et diverses elles aussi, à peine mieux connues. L'herbe haute, légère, qui tremble sans aucune apparence d'effroi ou seulement d'agitation, qui vibre plutôt, et c'est le soir, le long soir d'été où volent les martinets. Des iris d'eau fleurissent en jaune, des grenouilles commencent à coasser (plus tard, elles étonneront par le volume de leur voix). Un nid de roseaux tressés à fleur d'eau porte des oeufs ivoire tachés de brun ou de gris, on ne peut s'approcher, les berges sont traîtres. On pense à des histoires, à l'Histoire – si violente – en regardant l'herbe éternelle, frêle, qu'on va faucher, ou qui sèchera. Une abondance sans luxe, une foison sans opulence: je me doutais bien que j'allais m'empêtrer à son propos plus que jamais.

Encore une chose qui est donnée au passant comme un souffle.

Au-dessous des yeux, autour de nos pas, comme l'eau sur la grève qui touche les chevilles, de couleur plutôt sombre et sans éclat, un vert sourd (amical, peut-on dire intime? nullement étranger en tout cas), mais habité de fleurs elles-mêmes discrètes, modestes, presque pauvres, dédaignées et néanmoins nombreuses et gaies, sans beaucoup de parfum probablement (très différentes des riches fleurs de jardin), disons: presque insignifiantes et comme sans nom.

Une étendue animée, accueillante, rassurante, fraîche. La terre qui se modifie en surface, sous le ciel, qui se divise, s'allège, s'anime

May

I have spoken of the May meadow once before, a gay and fragile festival, but today it is not the same meadow, nor the same time of day; here there are several meadows, vaguer and vaster, seen not in bright sunlight but in the evening light; in a small valley where the land is drained but still damp and easily waterlogged, and where big bushes, growing wild but in regular shapes, seem to be floating like domes over a chorus of nightingales, between low walls and paths which are also grassy, under a grey sky.

Once again it is something that startles me as I pass by, strikes me like a soft and almost noiseless arrow, claims my attention – and I can already feel how difficult it will be to speak of it, because it is among the most unobtrusive, the most ordinary of things.

High, light, waving grasses of different species (which it would really serve no purpose to distinguish or to name), and amongst them, pink or yellow flowers, themselves indistinct, numerous and diverse, and hardly more familiar. The high, weightless grass trembling with no sign of fear or even agitation, but astir, and it is evening, the long summer evening with swifts flying. There are yellow water flags in bloom, frogs are starting to croak (later on the loudness of their voices will seem incredible). In a nest of plaited reeds on the surface of the water there are ivory-coloured eggs speckled brown or grey: it is impossible to get close because the banks are treacherous. Stories come to mind, the violent stories of History come to mind, as you watch the eternally frail grass which will either be scythed or grow parched. Abundance without ostentation, profusion without opulence: I was right to think that I would become more entangled than ever trying to express it.

Yet another gift for the passer-by, given like a breath.

Lower than the gaze, around our footsteps, like water lapping one's ankles on the sea-shore, there is a muted green, rather dark and lustreless (friendly, even intimate perhaps? certainly no stranger), but inhabited by flowers which are themselves unobtrusive, ordinary, almost poor, spurned yet numerous and gay, probably with little scent to them (very different from lavish garden flowers); let's say: almost insignificant, almost anonymous.

An animate landscape, welcoming, reassuring, fresh. Earth's changing surface beneath the sky, dividing, becoming lighter, enlivened,

et monte. On ne saurait parler d'un chant; à peine d'un chanton-
nement. Si près de nous. Si simple.

Le soir, la tranquillité encore claire du long soir, l'aisance du
grand ciel argenté où filent les oiseaux – le soleil étant couché, la
température douce, le vent sans violence – et un peu partout s'élève
le chant des rossignols cachés, si semblable à de l'eau qui ruisselle,
au bruit d'une fontaine exaltée; c'est comme si on marchait parmi
de nombreuses fontaines sans les voir, dans ce large vallon bordé
de chênes. Et le sol de tout cela, ce sont ces grands prés mobiles
mais silencieux, leur étendue vibrante habitée de fleurs anonymes,
un frémissement de tiges fines, droites, porteuses de graines, à peine
attachées à la terre bien que liées à sa noire profondeur. Comme si
la terre s'affinait en montant vers le ciel pur, lui tendait ces offrandes
sans poids, à la rencontre de la pluie, leur soeur.

Sur le moment, je n'ai noté que cela. Bien conscient qu'une
fois de plus je bâtissais ainsi une réalité à côté de l'autre ou autour
d'elle, qui en avait gardé quelques traits mais en cachait ou en
déformait d'autres et, de ce fait, découragé d'avance. M'avouant
par moments que le seul mot de «pré», ou mieux de «prairie», en
disait plus que ces recherches toujours menacées de préciosité.
M'obstinant tout de même aujourd'hui, après coup, donc peut-
être trop tard.

Du vert, oui, mais ni sombre, ni clair, à peine une couleur, plus
indistinct, plus effacé ou secret que celui des arbres.
De l'espace, au-dessous des yeux, autour des pas, lui aussi vague,
mais animé d'une vibration incessante, légère, tranquille, ne faisant
que peu de bruit, ou pas du tout.
Une multitude de choses fines, sans poids bien qu'enracinées
dans la terre, et porteuses de graines. Les «hautes herbes».
Il ne faut pas s'en approcher trop, on ne le peut pas, au fond.
Tout proche, cela reste infiniment lointain. Et malgré tout c'est
comme un don qui vous est fait, un accueil qui vous est offert.

moving upwards. It cannot be called a song; barely a humming voice. So close. So simple.

It is evening, the still clear tranquillity of the long evening, the ease of the wide silvered sky crossed by birds – when the sun has set and it is warm and the wind without violence – and almost everywhere there rises the song of hidden nightingales, so like streaming water or the sound made by a fountain at its full height; it is like walking amid numerous, unseen fountains, in this broad valley bordered by oak trees. And all this is grounded in broad meadows, in motion but silent, the quivering landscape inhabited by anonymous flowers, a shudder of thin, straight stalks, carrying their seeds, barely attached to the earth, yet tied to its dark depths. As if the earth were becoming purer as it rises to meet the pure sky, holding out these weightless offerings to it, going to meet the rain, their sister.

This was all I immediately noted. Fully aware once more that I was building up one kind of reality beside the other, or around it, retaining a few of its features but concealing or distorting others, and because of that, I was discouraged from the start. Admitting to myself now and then that the very word 'grass', or better still 'grassland', was more expressive than this seeking for words which runs the constant risk of preciosity.

Yet still obstinately pursuing the search today, after the event, and so possibly too late.

Green – yes – but neither dark nor light, scarcely a colour at all, less distinct, more effaced or hidden than the green of trees.

Space, lower than the gaze, around one's footsteps, itself only a vague impression, but alive with a ceaseless quivering, light, calm, almost noiseless, even silent.

A multitude of delicate, weightless things, yet things rooted in earth and carrying seeds. The 'high grasses'.

It is important not to come too close to all this, and, ultimately, it is impossible to do so. However close, it all remains infinitely remote. And yet, it is like a gift offered you, like a welcome.

143

Le soir, quand la source de la lumière, du jour, s'est recachée, avant la nuit. Le ciel argenté apparaît comme un immense miroir où les derniers oiseaux seraient les reflets d'autres oiseaux, des traces noires et rapides, sifflantes. Sous le ciel argenté, la lampe étant cachée, éloignée...

Et moi je marche dans ces lieux, je les traverse. Un homme menacé, comme les autres, dans ce vaste espace. Si je volais, ce serait à la manière effrayée et gauche des chauves-souris. Pourtant, je suis reçu, accueilli dans ces prairies. Les dieux depuis longtemps se détournent. Nous n'avions plus la force de les porter. Les vases de libation sont couchés en débris sous la terre, tels des coeurs qui ont trop contenu. L'avernir effarouche nos derniers feux. On est comme quelqu'un qui n'arrive pas au bout d'une phrase commencée.

(Faut-il vraiment remonter aux dieux pour dire cela?)

Y a-t-il un lien du vert avec la nuit? de l'herbe avec la nuit?

Quelques couleurs, quelques fleurs là-dedans, roses, bleues, jaunes, petites.

Vert et argent. Hautes herbes le soir, prés avant la nuit. Entre le jour et la nuit. Pas besoin de soleil, au contraire. Un répit. Est-ce comme un sommeil? Un lit qui invite à s'y étendre ?

Encore une chose intermédiaire, tellement proche et tellement lointaine, comme si elle n'avait pas seulement un corps.

Flèches qui bougent doucement dans le carquois de pierre.

Sous le ciel argenté comme un immense miroir où les derniers oiseaux seraient des reflets sifflants, violents, d'autre chose.

Les prés chantonnent à ras de terre contre la mort; ils disent l'air, l'espace, ils murmurent que l'air vit, que la terre continue à respirer.

Evening: when the source of light, of day, has hidden itself once more, before nightfall. The silvered sky appears to be an immense mirror in which the last birds are the reflections of other birds, rapid black traces, whistling by. Beneath the silvered sky, with the lamp hidden, distanced...

And I walk in these places, I pass through them. A threatened man, as others are, in this vast space. If I could fly, I should fly with the frightened clumsiness of a bat. Yet in these meadows I am received, welcomed. The gods have turned aside from them long ago. We no longer had the strength to support them. The libation jars lie asleep in shattered fragments under the earth like hearts that have borne too much. The future scares off the last of our fire. We are like people who cannot get to the end of a sentence.

(Do the gods really have to be invoked just to say this?)

Is there a link between green and the night? between grass and the night?

A few colours, a few flowers there too, pink, blue, yellow...tiny.

Green and silver. High grasses in the evening, meadows before nightfall. Between day and night. No need of the sun, quite the contrary. A respite. Like sleep? Like a bed just asking you to lie down upon it?

Once again something intermediary, so close yet so remote, as if it had no body at all.

Arrows gently stirring in the stone quiver.

Beneath the sky silvered over like an immense mirror in which the last birds are the whistling, violent reflections of something else.

The meadows hum a song on the earth's surface, a song directed against death; they speak of the air, of space, they murmur that the air is alive, that the earth goes on breathing.

Je n'ai jamais su prier, je suis incapable d'aucune prière.

Là, entre le jour et la nuit, quand le porteur du jour s'est éloigné derrière les montagnes, il me semble que les prés pourraient être une prière à voix très basse, une sorte de litanie distraite et rassurante comme le bruit d'un ruisseau, soumise aux faibles impulsions de l'air.

Je ne veux pas pour autant m'agenouiller en ce lieu, ni même prétendre que je me suis trouvé là sur des traces divines. Ce serait une autre espèce d'erreur. Je peux à peine préciser tout cela. Mais ces prairies existent, dispersées. Il ne faut même pas les chercher. On les longe à la fin d'une journée, de n'importe quelle journée, quand la lumière se fait moins distincte, le pas plus lent, et c'est comme s'il y avait une ombre à côté de vous revenue d'infiniment loin, alors qu'on ne l'espérait plus, et qui, si on se retournait pour la voir, ne s'effacerait peut-être même pas.

I have never known how to pray. I am incapable of any prayer.

There, between day and night, when the carrier of daylight has disappeared behind the mountains, it seems to me that the meadows could be a low-voiced prayer, a kind of distracted litany, as comforting as the sound of a stream, subjected to the gentle impetus of the air.

That is no reason for me to kneel down in this place or to claim that I have discovered the traces of the gods here. That would be another kind of mistake. I can scarcely say anything precise about all this. Yet these fields exist, in dispersion. There is not even any need to seek them out. You walk along by them at the end of a day, any day, as the light dims, as the footsteps slow down, and it is as if there were a shadow at your side which has returned from somewhere infinitely far away, when you no longer expected it, and which, should you turn to see it, would perhaps not even disappear.

STARLINGS
ÉTOURNEAUX

Soudain, alors qu'on marchait distraitement, paisiblement, en amicale compagnie, dans la combe déserte (qui n'est peuplée que de roseaux et d'herbes), sous le haut ciel en train de s'argenter, cette légère rumeur de flèches très haut dans l'air vous fait dresser la tête, interdits. D'où venue? Et non moins soudainement, l'on aperçoit à l'endroit du bruit comme un très rapide nuage, non, une chose trop prompte pour être un nuage, et qui à tout moment passe du noir au gris, du mat au brillant, change de forme, se désagrège, s'efface...

Plutôt qu'un nuage, des nuages – car il y en a presque tout de suite plusieurs, infatigables dans leur course bruissante – on dirait des fumées; c'est à présent au-dessus des collines boisées tout un feu d'artifice de fumées qui tracent des boucles dans le ciel, les ouvrent, les ferment, les resserrent, les dénouent, les emmêlent, qui explosent en grandes ombelles de suie, se perdent au plus haut du ciel en traînées, en cendre; ou au contraire descendent presque à ras des crêtes, plus bas même, et alors on pense à de grands filets à mailles serrées jetés par des pêcheurs sur les chênes, rapidement retirés, vides, et remontés.

Ou à des bannières sombres qu'on ne sait qui fait flotter, brandit, déploie, escamote – sombres sans être funèbres: trop frémissantes, trop vibrantes, trop claquantes pour cela.

Troupes vraiment électrisées par leur rassemblement, par leur seul nombre qui paraît à chaque minute moins dénombrable; et maintenant le bruit de flèches s'intensifie – ou c'est comme le vent quand il souffle dans les roseaux secs avec violence, cela vient de très loin, vous traverse, vous communique sa fièvre sans qu'on ait presque le temps de rien comprendre...

L'étrange fête dure longtemps; puis se produit une espèce d'accalmie; de grandes troupes sont devenues bientôt invisibles derrière la crête des bois ou trop haut dans le ciel moins lumineux; et la plus proche descendant en direction des roseaux de l'étang (depuis longtemps asséché), flottant telle une longue fumée au-dessus d'eux, se défait enfin en autant de flocons de suie qui tombent, plus lentement cette fois, mais régulièrement, un à un, dans ce grand frémissement de paille où ils disparaissent, tandis que s'élève de ces fourrés un bavardage effréné, véritable crépitement...

Suddenly – as you were walking along distractedly, peaceably, with friends, in the deserted hollow (there is nothing apart from reeds and grasses), beneath a tall sky turning to silver – the soft whirring of arrows high in the air makes you look up, startled. Where did it come from? Then, no less suddenly, in the place where the noise was, you notice something like a very swift cloud – but no, it was too sudden to be a cloud – and it constantly changes from black to grey, from dullness to brilliance, reshaping itself, disintegrating, disappearing ...

Rather than a cloud, or clouds – because, almost immediately, there are several of them in an indefatigable, whirring race – you might say that they were like wisps of smoke; and now, above the wooded hills, there is a whole firework display, wisps of smoke tracing loops in the sky, opening, closing, tightening, unwinding, merging, then exploding into huge sooty umbels before they disappear high up in the sky, in trails, into ashes; or else they come down and skim the hill crests, or even lower, and call to mind huge webs of close-meshed netting cast by fishermen over the oak trees, rapidly hauled back – empty – and hoisted up again.

Or dark banners waved by one unknown, flourished, unfurled, conjured away: dark, but not dismal: too quivering, too vibrant, flapping too noisily for that.

Troops literally charged with electricity in the way they rally together, by their sheer number – and that number is harder to count by the minute; and now the whirr of arrows intensifies – or seems like a wind blowing violently among the dry reeds; it all comes from somewhere very far away, shoots through you and communicates its frenzied excitement almost before you have time to grasp what is happening...

The strange display lasts a long time; there follows a kind of lull; the massed troops have soon been lost to sight behind the crest of the woods, or too high in the sky which is now less luminous; the nearest troop flies down towards the reed bed on the pond (long since dried up), floating above them like a long wisp of smoke, and finally scatters into so many flakes of soot, falling more slowly this time but in a regular pattern, one by one, into the huge shuddering of dried stalks where they disappear, while from the dense clumps of reeds there rises a frenzied chit-chat, a positive crackle of sound...

Le silence s'est refait. Encore un peu, et l'on n'y verra plus très clair. On est comme quelqu'un qui quitte à regret le lieu d'une fête, émerveillé et un peu triste que ce soit, déjà, fini.

(Je ne puis m'empêcher de déceler dans ce que j'ai écrit là un peu d'artifice – qu'il faudrait franchir, que peut-être je ne saurai plus franchir. Probablement parce qu'on est trop loin de ces oiseaux – et aussi, de soi-même. Je me fais l'effet d'un prestidigitateur d'ailleurs maladroit que l'on inviterait à rengainer son matériel pour montrer enfin, après ces leurres, une chose vraie, étrangère à toute scène, à tout théâtre. Comment faire pour que le promeneur ne se mue pas en spectateur et, ensuite, en montreur? Il faudrait être mêlé de plus près au monde, avoir avec lui des liens plus nécessaires.)

On est tout à coup cerné par un vol ultra-rapide de flèches obscures, sorties toutes à la fois d'innombrables carquois. Ainsi le vent venu du nord traverse les roseaux de paille, ainsi l'espace vient à vous, ainsi l'air laboure les prés. C'est comme si quelqu'un accourait à votre aide, une messagère, Iris, de très loin et du plus frais du monde venue vous rejoindre, – c'est presque la jeunesse qui vous rattrape et déjà vous dépasse, pieds nus, odorante, dans sa robe d'air…Et l'on ne halète plus, on se redresse, on serait près de courir, si l'on pouvait, après cette coureuse…

Une fête à deux pas, et tellement loin.
Une fête de suie, de fumée, et nulle part on ne discerne le feu d'où elle a dû surgir. C'est que nous ne sommes pas des oiseaux. Et nous devons hâter le pas pour être de retour avant la nuit.
Non sans avoir toutefois ensemble, quelques-uns, tendu les mains en souriant au-dessus de l'invisible feu.

The silence has returned. In a while it will be difficult to see much at all. It feels like a reluctant parting from a scene of festivity, you are full of wonder yet slightly disappointed that it has, already, come to an end.

(I cannot help detecting in what I have written so far an element of contrivance – I need to go beyond that, but perhaps I no longer know how. Possibly because we are too far removed from these birds – and from ourselves. I strike myself as some sort of conjurer, and a clumsy one at that, who has been invited to pack away his tricks and to get down to showing something real after all his illusionism, something that has nothing at all to do with scenery and theatres. What can be done to prevent the walker from turning into a spectator and then into a puppeteer? It would mean being involved more closely with the world, having less random links with it.)

You are suddenly encircled by an ultra-rapid flight of dark arrows, all of them released at once from countless quivers. This is the way the north wind shoots through the dead reeds, the way space comes towards you and the air ploughs the fields. It is as if someone were hurrying to help you, a messenger, Iris, come to rejoin you from far far away, from the freshest part of the world – almost like youth catching up with you and overtaking you already, barefoot, sweet-smelling, in a mantle of air...You no longer gasp for breath, you get up, almost ready to break into a run, were it possible, in pursuit of this sweet pursuer...

A festival a stone's throw away, yet so distant.
A festival of soot and smoke with no sign of the fire from which it must have sprung. Because we are not birds. We must press on if we are to get back before dark.
But not before a few of us, smiling, have stretched out our hands above the invisible fire.

153

Bloodaxe Contemporary French Poets

Series Editors: Timothy Mathews & Michael Worton

FRENCH-ENGLISH BILINGUAL EDITIONS

'Bloodaxe's Contemporary French Poets series could not have arrived at a more opportune time, and I cannot remember any translation initiative in the past thirty years that has been more ambitious or more coherently planned in its attempt to bring French poetry across the Channel and the Atlantic. Under the editorship of Timothy Mathews and Michael Worton, the series has a clear format and an even clearer sense of mission' – MALCOLM BOWIE, *TLS*

159

Printed in the USA
CPSIA information can be obtained
at www.ICGtesting.com
JSHW082211140824
68134JS00014B/558